If you are thinking ~~~~
get all your questions answered before you decide.

QUESTIONS THIS BOOK WILL ANSWER FOR YOU:

- What does a mortgage broker do?
- How does a mortgage broker make money?
- What is a mortgage broker?
- What is a typical day like?
- Do I need a license?
- How do I get my license?
- So why do lenders work with mortgage brokers?
- How do I get the training I need?
- How much can I earn?
- Can I work from home?
- So what exactly does a mortgage broker do?
- How do I decide what company to work for?
- How do I open my own company?
- How do I find lenders to work with?
- Is my job secure?
- Can I do this part time?
- How do I get started?
- What do I do first?
- How long does it take to start?

- What do I have to know?
- What exactly does the processor do?
- What does an underwriter do?
- How do I know if I will be a good broker?
- What is an appraiser?
- Where do I get the credit reports?
- What does the title company do?
- How do people choose their broker?
- What about the competition?
- How do I get clients?
- What exactly is mortgage banking?
- What is continuing education?
- What does the future of the industry look like?
- How do I motivate myself?
- Aren't mortgages a seasonal business?
- How do I hide my inexperience?
- **And many more...**

WHAT OTHERS ARE SAYING . . .

❝This book really helped me save hours of running around trying to find answers. Everything I wanted to know was in your book, and because of it I was able to get into the business much sooner than I expected. ❞

—Rick Sanchez • Houston, Tx

❝I had been looking for a new job for a while. I was laid off after 13 years. Your book helped me decide and helped me get started quickly. It really made a difference. Becoming a mortgage broker was a great decision. ❞

—Douglas Robinson • Springfield

❝At first, I thought this book was going to be an advertisement to become a mortgage broker. Boy, was I wrong. You covered the good and the bad. Some people might read this and even decide this business is not for them. And if that is the case, it is better they find out before they get involved. Too many new brokers think all you do is fill out paperwork. They do not understand the complexities involved. Your book gives an real inside view of the business. ❞

—Samantha Poole • San Diego, California

66 I loved *So You Want To Be A Mortgage Broker.* I'm looking for a new career path and my sister-in-law suggested becoming a mortgage broker. I knew nothing about it. Your book gave me all the information that I needed about starting in the business and insights of what I need to do to succeed. There are no other books like this out in circulation. 99
—**Mary Kay Reed Clearwater Fl**

66 The book, *So You Want To Be A Mortgage Broker* provides very helpful information to the beginner and the person interested in learning about the exciting and potentially profitable field of home finance. The author, Ameen Kamadia, lays out the information in simple and plain language and provides the reader with pragmatic information and tips which can be applied in the real 'mortgage world.' 99
—**Alan Abergel, J.D., California Mortgage Broker**

66 *So You Want To Be a Mortgage Broker* has not only answered all my questions, but has instilled me with informed motivation! Words can't express how grateful I am, to have come across your website. Your book reassured my decision to begin working as a loan officer last week. I've made plans to get my Mortgage Broker license soon. I am lucky enough to start out with my very own office, working with a family friend who is a mortgage broker with two office locations. Obviously I'm going to have to get RMLOME soon, along with the marketing information you provide. My friend has been working very hard and I can't wait to lead them to your website so that they can start 'working very smart'!

God bless your desire to help others achieve their successful potential Ameen. I will continue to inform you of my progress! You and all the wonderful people in your company are AWESOME!! 99
Truthfully,
—**Sylvia Bisker**

66 Well I was information seeking when I came across your website. After reading what was there I got more curious, I already have a job as a loan officer and being new to this profession I wanted to learn as much as possible. Everything I got from your book was inspirational and made me feel like I could do this, I can be a Mortgage Broker and be very successful. I feel that with what you teach and you in my corner, I cant do anything BUT be successful.

THANK YOU SO MUCH for being there for those of us just getting started, and sharing your wisdom and teachings! 99
—Lady Melody J. Clancy

66 I really have enjoyed the book. It has so much information to answer all of my questions. It gave me the step by step process to starting my Mortgage Broker business. I was so impressed with the information in the book, not to mention, all of the on-line help and tech support that I need is just right at my fingertips. Thanks sooooo much. 99
—Tammy Standifer, Oklahoma

66 I am 48 years young and looking to get into the mortgage business…I bought your book, *So You Want To Be a Mortgage Broker*. I know this is going to sound scripted but I LOVED THE BOOK!! I read it in 5 hours…couldn't put it down…read and re-read and so on…it was so interesting and educational that I went and ordered your training book.

Just so happens that I met with the President of a local mortgage company today to put myself in position to start getting business and knowing where to send it. I have previously met with this President about getting into the business but that was prior to reading your book.

Well to say the least I felt like I knew the business just from reading *So You Want To Be a Mortgage Broker*, so my meeting today was much better because I actually understood much of what he was saying to me. And I knew what to ask him too. 99
—Mario Evangelist, Philadelphia PA

SO YOU WANT TO BE A MORTGAGE BROKER

AMEEN KAMADIA
KAMROCK PUBLISHING

Dedicated to my father for getting me into this great business. Thanks, Dad, for continuing to push and encourage me everyday.

If you are truly serious about the mortgage profession, there is a FREE resource you must become familiar with. It is called Mortgage Magic.

This tool will teach you more than you ever dreamed of knowing regarding marketing, mortgages, borrowers, and everything related.

SOME OF THE THINGS YOU WILL LEARN ARE:

- How to increase your customers' credit scores.
- How to spend less money on marketing and get better results.
- How to have Realtors eating out of your hand.
- The proper method to follow up with leads and double your income.
- How to automate your marketing.
- What factors cause homebuyers to choose one lender over another. And it's not the price!
- How to make your prospects an offer they can't refuse.
- And a lot more.

All this is brought to you FREE from the publisher of this book. All you have to do is visit the following website:

http://www.MortgageMagic.info

WHY THIS BOOK WAS WRITTEN:

My company, Kamrock Publishing, has a web site called **www.mortgagebrokertraining.com**. This is our main site for mortgage professionals. We have several training and marketing resources available at this site.

But what we didn't have was a way to help people get into the mortgage business. And every day we received multiple emails from people wanting to know how to get a license, where to start, how to find a company to work for, etc.

And after a while, we got tired of answering these emails, so we put together the only book available that shows people how to get into the business. That book is in your hands right now.

If you have any questions about what to do to become a mortgage broker, or if you want a behind-the-scenes look at the world of mortgage brokerage, this book will be invaluable to you.

TABLE OF CONTENTS

CHAPTER 1

Introduction:
A New World

So you want to be a mortgage broker?

Or maybe you're not sure yet.

Let's imagine a little.

Imagine a world where you are your own master. You have the time to do whatever you wish. You have the ability to live up to your true potential. No limits, no barriers. No handicaps or favoritism or discrimination. Nothing can hold you back. You can be as successful as you wish. Your income is limited only by your desire.

And the work is good too. No menial labor required. You can work whenever you want, wherever you wish. No time clocks to punch or bosses to bother you. No formal education required. Just be yourself. Your success is based on honesty and integrity.

You live in a respectable, white-collar universe. Computers, cell phones, and air-conditioned offices are your domain. High finance is your game.

Your market is virtually unlimited. Everyone wants and needs your product: Money.

And they will do what it takes to get it.

You are living a comfortable, luxurious lifestyle with no more financial worries. But the beauty of it is: You didn't need any money to get started. So you never had anything to risk. From the very start, the money belonged to someone else. You made money by helping them distribute it.

This is the world of the mortgage broker. A world you can join, if you have what it takes to make a decision. This is not a new opportunity. It has been around since there was money. And it will continue to be around as long as man walks the earth.

The trails are well worn. You don't need to forge new territory here. Thousands of successful brokers have walked this way before. And all you have to do is follow their path. No guesswork. No risk.

The only question is, will you be a part of it?

LIFE AS A MORTGAGE BROKER

Ask yourself this: What is it you desire out of life?

- More money?

- Financial security?

- A good future for your family?

- A chance to help others?

- Freedom?

All these can be yours, easily. If thousands of regular, everyday people can do it, so can you.

Mortgage brokerage is one of the last remaining businesses in which you are judged by your output, not by who you know, or where you went to school. In fact, it doesn't matter if you went to school at all. It might actually be better if you didn't.

Your income is unlimited. No external factors can stop you. You alone determine your success.

If you ever thought you could do great things, this is the opportunity to show that you can.

You don't need any money to get started. You don't even need a computer. All you need is the belief that you can succeed and the desire to make it happen.

Imagine how it feels to get a hug from a man and a woman, who have just bought their first house—a dream they've cherished for years—one made possible only because you were there to help them.

That is the life of a mortgage broker. And this book will fill you in on all the details of this life: both the good and the bad.

THE TIME IS NOW

The mortgage profession, more than ever before, faces a future marked by expanding technology, digital marketing, specialized knowledge, and growing marketplaces. The fast-paced, complex and constantly changing market holds the promise of success for those with the drive to achieve. Hard work, intelligent effort, and a positive spirit can turn your dreams into reality.

The journey is not easy, but the rewards are many. Personal determination and commitment are key factors. Fortunately, Kamrock Publishing, MoneyTree Mortgage, your local area Association of Mortgage Brokers, and National Association of

Mortgage Brokers (NAMB) are standing by with training, knowledge, support, and guidance to help you succeed in this exciting career.

Read on to discover the opportunities that await you in the world of finance. Join the thousands of professionals who have decided to make mortgage brokerage a lifetime career. Find out why so many have achieved personal career goals, built solid reputations, enjoyed the respect of their peers, and received the rightful rewards of diligently serving the public.

Now is the time for you to join tomorrow's pacesetters in an expanding marketplace that offers so many possibilities.

This career path can be a lifetime pursuit for the adventuresome. Few limits exist for those who understand its true potential.

A career in real estate finance encompasses more than simply the mechanics of taking loan applications. It's about helping people, providing families with homes, furnishing investors with security, helping new entrepreneurs find opportunities, and, ultimately, building better communities for the future.

The world is driven by real estate. It is the American Dream to own a home, and mortgage professionals are vital to that process. Every day, thousands of brokers make dreams come true from Key West to Seattle. Somewhere, at this moment, mortgage brokers are assisting buyers in making the largest single purchase that they may ever undertake.

Most brokers will tell you there's nothing quite like the emotional and, of course, the financial satisfaction that comes from the successful negotiation of a real estate transaction. Few regret making a career choice that is really a way of life. Enter a world that offers career flexibility, financial paybacks, and great growth potential.

WHAT IT TAKES TO SUCCEED

Of course, like anything that offers such rich rewards, a successful career in real estate finance doesn't just happen. Success requires hard work and rarely comes easily. But the good news is, if you're willing to work hard, your success is virtually guaranteed.

Mortgage brokerage is also extremely demanding. A personal commitment to excellence is essential. Those who enter the profession will reap great rewards, but they will travel down a long and challenging road to get there.

From the outset, be prepared to invest your time in a life-long learning exercise. Completing required courses is just the beginning of a journey continuously fuelled by the newest and most effective skills. The market is dynamic, legislation is constantly changing, and new technologies are continuously emerging. Little wonder that knowledge is power in the real estate marketplace.

As with any great success, personal sacrifices are a reality. At the eleventh hour, stakes are high and loans must close. Critics point to long hours, high stress levels, and reduced social life. Proponents argue it's all a matter of perspective and balance. Trade-offs must be made, but the personal freedom, the opportunity for a satisfying career, and the long-term benefits are well worth the effort.

A career in finance is anything but routine. Sales representatives are constantly in and out of the office making contacts, procuring loans, visiting clients, and negotiating agreements. Even better, no two transactions are ever the same; variety is truly the spice of life.

Many attributes and skills contribute to success in real estate. Experience indicates that certain talents, qualities, and personal traits can improve the odds of building a worthwhile career.

- **Math skills**—a basic grounding in math fundamentals, with proficiency in multiplication, division, fractions, and amortization. These skills are required when calculating payments, as well as calculating ratios and setting interest rates.

- **Research skills**—a practical knowledge of how to locate, read, and understand legal documents. Familiarity with basic document structures will assist when researching materials concerning property ownership.

- **Organization/Planning skills**—an ability to organize personal affairs as well as conduct business activity in a logical, efficient manner. These qualities are useful in marketing, interviewing clients, placing the loan, and conducting the closing.

- **Computer knowledge**—a fundamental understanding of computer hardware and software. Computer use is increasingly commonplace both in internal brokerage operations, as well as in property searches. Long-term success is directly tied to technological competencies.

- **Negotiating ability**—an important factor in any business transaction. Loan officers are routinely called upon to negotiate on behalf of the borrower or lender to arrive at mutually agreeable terms.

- **Interview techniques**—a basic understanding of questioning methods. Real estate success often depends on asking the right question at the right time. This skill is most valued in situations involving buyers and the determination of their purchasing needs.

- **Rapport**—the hallmark of the successful loan officer. Rapport is the ability to establish relationships of mutual trust. Real estate is best suited to individuals who enjoy working with people, taking interest in their well-being, and quickly understanding their needs and wants.

- **Self-Starter**—the ability to get the job done. Real estate financing demands discipline, self-motivation, and personal commitment.

Certain practical realities face anyone contemplating this career. Generating loans will undoubtedly be the most important function performed every day. Lead generation, a challenge for most people, demands a systematic approach, along with perseverance and determination.

Successful loan officers develop a clientele based on a solid reputation, built with diligence, honesty, and integrity. Initially, referrals may arise from friends, relatives, or acquaintances.

In the beginning, some opportunities may develop more out of coincidence than planned marketing, but never overlook the need to set your course carefully. Career-minded brokers are always building an ever-expanding sphere of influence to ensure long-term client awareness and retention.

This is a very exciting field, but don't underestimate the challenge. The first years are demanding, while new contacts are being made. Over time, the hectic pace gives way to more predictable and reliable sources of business through referrals and repeat customers.

Monetary rewards in this profession are closely aligned to sales ability and people skills, but few guarantees exist as to ultimate income. While financial uncertainty is a reality, you enjoy the opportunity of getting out of mortgage brokerage much more than what you put in.

PUTTING SYSTEMS IN PLACE

That does not mean that there is no way to make as much as you want. The easiest way to achieve your financial goals is by implementing proper systems. You cannot fly by the seat of your pants all the time. By using systems in your business, you can set it up to work automatically—whether you are there or not.

For example, there are systems to attract clients. There are systems to pre-qualify them. There are systems to attract Realtor partners. There are systems to do follow up. And there are systems to stay in touch with past clients.

Systems make it possible to reach the upper levels of production. You alone can only do so much. A lot of your work should be automated.

Once you start doing well, you will need to hire help. Hiring assistants is very difficult for new brokers, since they think they can do a better job themselves. But only by employing others can you grow your business. And having help allows you to focus on the things that are most important and the aspects of the business you enjoy the most.

CHAPTER 2

What is a Mortgage Broker?

- **WHAT DOES A BROKER DO?**
- **HOW DOES A BROKER MAKE MONEY?**

WHAT IS A MORTGAGE BROKER?

The official definition from the National Association of Mortgage Brokers is this:

> *A mortgage broker is an independent real estate financing professional who specializes in the origination of residential and/or commercial mortgages. Mortgage brokers normally pass on the actual funding and servicing of loans to capital sources who act as loan "wholesalers."*

There are thousand of mortgage brokerage operations across the nation. They originate over half of all residential loans in the U.S.

According to a study in 2003 by the well-known research firm Wholesale Access:

- There were over 44,000 mortgage brokerages in the country.

- They accounted for $1.69 trillion in loans (65% of all loans).

- The average company did $38.3 million in loans and had 10 employees.

A mortgage broker is also an independent contractor working, on average, with 40 wholesale lenders at any one time. By combining professional expertise with direct access to hundreds of loan products, a broker provides consumers the most efficient and cost-effective method of offering suitable financing options tailored to the consumer's specific financial goals.

The term "mortgage broker" can be used to describe a person or a company. In most states, if you say mortgage broker, you are talking about a company. The actual people who work there are loan officers. But the term is interchangeable. A loan officer can call himself a mortgage broker, even if he is not licensed as one.

Mortgage brokers help people get mortgage loans. They act as middlemen in the transaction. Consumers come to them, because they work with many different lenders, each with many different loans programs, options, and rates. The mortgage broker can effectively "shop" the consumer's loan around to different lenders on behalf of the consumer. And because of the broker's expertise, he can recommend the best loan.

If there were no mortgage brokers, consumers would have to physically go to several banks and lenders, apply with each of them, understand their loan programs, compare the rates and fees charged by each, and decide which lender to get the loan from. This could take days of needless drudgery.

A mortgage broker is like a car dealership that sells every make and model car you could ask for. No need to drive around from dealer to dealer to check out similar cars. They are all in one place.

WHAT IS A TYPICAL DAY LIKE?

A mortgage broker is free to start and stop his day whenever he wants. A new mortgage broker should have the discipline to put in the time needed to get his career off the ground. There are two main activities mortgage brokers engage in:

1. Prospecting

2. Customer Service

Prospecting involves getting new customers. This is the most important thing you can do. Never, ever stop prospecting. No matter how successful you are, if you stop prospecting, eventually your business will dry up and you will be out of business.

Every successful broker spends time every day generating leads and following up on existing leads.

A senior trainer at a national mortgage company tells all his students that if they can get one meeting a day with a potential loan applicant, they can take the rest of the day off.

For their service, mortgage brokers have to charge fees. The most common is the Origination Fee. This is usually 1% of the loan amount, and makes the bulk of the commission earned by the mortgage broker. But even lenders charge this fee, so a consumer is going to pay it, whether he goes to a mortgage broker or a lender.

Most of the time, a consumer can get a better deal from a broker than from a lender. This is because brokers work on commission. If they do not do a loan, they do not eat, so they are much more willing to negotiate with a consumer than a lender. Since loan officers working for lenders are typically on salary, they do not need to do as many loans to make the same amount of money.

Mortgage brokers can also set their own criteria. Lenders already have strict policies set in place. If a borrower does not want or cannot pay for an application fee, the lender will say "Sorry, have a nice day." On the other hand, a broker might be willing to waive the application fee if the loan is worth doing.

SO WHY DO LENDERS WORK WITH MORTGAGE BROKERS?

Money. Mortgage brokers serve as an extension of the lender. Lenders can attract only a limited number of people with their marketing budgets. Mortgage brokers use their own marketing money, talent, contacts, and relationships to bring borrowers to themselves. If the mortgage broker sends a loan to a lender, the lender does not have to do very much to get that loan.

When each loan earns the lender several thousands of dollars, it does not make sense for a lender to avoid working with mortgage brokers. And many lenders do both. They have wholesale divisions, which concentrate on generating loans from mortgage brokers, and they have retail divisions, which work to get loans from consumers. It is not out of place for a consumer to go to a retail branch of a lender and get a higher rate quote than from a mortgage broker, who is going to send the loan to that same lender.

For example, Countrywide has both retail and wholesale divisions. Each is separate and operates independently. So if Borrower Bob goes to the Countrywide office and gets a loan rate quote of 7%, he could go to a mortgage broker and get a loan rate quote for the same Countrywide loan at 6.5%. It happens all the time. The reason is that the retail division adds its own commissions to the loan. It does the same job as the mortgage broker, but it can only offer loans of one lender.

There have also been cases where the retail division would offer a better deal to a consumer just to get the loan. Behind the scenes there are quotas, productions schedules, bonuses for production, and so on. So a retail division loan officer might do a loan without making any money upfront just to get the loan, and earn some special reward.

HOW DOES A MORTGAGE BROKER MAKE MONEY?

There are two primary ways mortgage brokers make money. They get paid from the borrower and they get paid from the lender. It sounds sneaky—and some mortgage brokers use this ability to really stick it to the borrower—but the majority use this as an added tool to offer the borrower what he needs. In the end, the borrower is the one paying for everything.

Let me explain.

Mortgage brokers get paid by borrowers in the form of fees. There are many different fees a mortgage broker could charge for just about anything he can think of. The most common ones are:

- Origination Fee

- Application Fee

- Mortgage-Broker Fee

- Processing Fee

These are fees that are charged to the borrower and are included in the closing costs. The borrower must bring this money to the closing table. All of these fees should be disclosed to the borrower in what is called a Good Faith Estimate. This is a federally required document outlining the estimated costs of the loan, so the borrower can compare loan charges from different places.

When a mortgage broker gets paid by the lender, it is called a Yield Spread Premium (YSP). Mortgage lenders offer many different loan programs. Each program has many different available interest rates based on a zillion factors: how large is the loan, how is the borrower's credit, when will the loan close, is it a first mortgage or a second, etc.

So mortgage brokers use rate sheets, which show the daily rate of the lender for each loan program and each scenario. Interest rates change on a daily basis and even sometimes more often.

If, for example, Borrower Bob is looking for an 80% Loan To Value (LTV; the amount of the loan compared to the purchase price or value of the house), and has perfect credit, the best rate he could get from Lender 1 is 6%, from Lender 2 is 6.25%, from Lender 3 is 6.5%, and from Lender 4 is 6.5%.

All of these rates are "at par," meaning there is no discount to be paid for this rate nor is there a YSP. If the mortgage broker convinces Borrower Bob to get a loan at 8%, that is 2% higher than the lowest rate available from Lender 1. If Borrower Bob goes through with this loan, the lender will pay the mortgage broker several points (percentage of the loan), because the lender will make a heck of a lot more money on the loan than it anticipated. The lender was happy to do the loan at 6%, but it gets to do it at 8%. Over the life of the loan, that adds up to tens of thousands of dollars in extra interest.

Now this example was a little extreme. Very rarely is any borrower so naïve as to accept a loan a full 2% higher than the norm. This almost never happens with "conforming loans" (loans for people with good credit and enough down payment).

This happens much more often in sub-prime loans. These are loans to people with bad credit or little money down. Lenders have more risk in lending money to these borrowers, so they charge more. Very few lenders work with people with really bad credit. So those mortgage brokers who can do these loans can essentially charge whatever rate they want, because they know the borrower cannot get this loan anywhere else— especially since the majority of sub-prime lenders do not have retail divisions. They do not work with the public, only with mortgage brokers.

Let's take another example. Recently, homebuilders have begun to own and operate their own mortgage companies. In order to entice people to use their own mortgage company, they give thousands away in upgrades to homebuyers.

How do they do this? First of all, $1,000 in upgrades is not worth $1,000. Homebuilders have an amazing mark-up when it comes to upgrades. That $1,000 in upgrades might cost them $100. So if they offer $10,000 in upgrades we are really talking about $1,000.

But homebuilders are in business to make money, so you know they will get this money out of the buyer somehow. And they get it from the YSP. Builder mortgage companies, almost all the time, offer borrowers higher interest rates than they can get from any mortgage broker. But the borrower sees thousands in free upgrades and decides it is worth paying a few dollars extra per month, so he gets the loan from the builder. The builder, of course, gets the $1,000 back, plus more, by charging a higher rate and pocketing the difference.

It is also common for mortgage brokers to advertise loans with no fees. But there is always a catch. The catch here is that the rate will be higher. A mortgage broker has to eat, right? If he doesn't get it from the borrower in fees, then he will get it from a higher rate.

So either way, the borrower pays. He can pay the fees upfront. Or he can pay more interest over the life of the loan.

We can't really say how much the average broker makes per loan. The statistics available on this are suspect. And it depends mainly on what homes are worth in your area. But we can try to figure it out.

As of early 2004, the average-priced house in the U.S. is worth over $170,000. The average Origination Fee is 1% of the loan amount. With a 10% down payment, a borrower would be getting a loan for $153,000. So that equals $1,530 as the Origination Fee. There also might be a $100 Application Fee. There will be a Processing Fee, let's say $400. And there might be a small YSP, let's say .75% ($1,147.50), for a grand total of $3,177.50.

Now the individual mortgage broker does not get to keep the whole commission (unless you own the company, in which case you do get to keep it all). Every company is different, but most brokers work on a commission split with their company. A 50% commission split is common.

The company sets the fees to charge. The broker usually gets a split of the Origination Fee, plus the YSP. So, in the above example, the company and the individual mortgage broker split $2,677.50. Assuming a 50% split, the mortgage broker would get $1,338.75. The company would keep the Application Fee and the Processing Fee. Now remember, this varies with every company.

There are also other fees that can be added to increase the bottom line. This example dealt with a perfect-credit applicant doing a conforming loan. Many loans are non-conforming, and the fees are much higher.

HOW MUCH CAN I EARN?

How much do you want to earn? Your earning potential is unlimited. Mortgage brokers originate over a trillion dollars worth of loans every year. You can have as much of this pie as you want. The top mortgage brokers originate over $100 million of loans every year.

There are thousands of people in this line of work and they are all making a living, or else they wouldn't be doing it.

It is not uncommon for an average broker to earn at least $60,000 a year in commissions. If you earn $1,500 per loan, you only need 3 loans a month to reach this level. How many loans you do is in direct correlation with how many leads you get. The more people you talk to about mortgages the more loans you will have.

On average, a mortgage broker converts 1 out of 4 leads into an application. So to do 3 loans a month, you need 12 leads a month. Do you think you can find 12 people a month who are either buying a home or need money from their home by refinancing?

Most probably, yes!

Once you get into the business, you will see what other brokers do to attract borrowers. Some of these marketing techniques work. Some do not. The broker with the most leads gets the most borrowers. But the great thing is, you do not need a whole bunch of borrowers.

If, instead of 12 people a month, you find 24 people a month (that's less than 1 per day) who need a loan, you will make more than $100,000!

Or you can increase the amount you make per loan. It is not like real estate, where you have a fixed commission of 6%. You can charge as much or as little as you wish. The more expensive the home, the more you make. The more difficult the loan—bad credit, high LTV, undocumented income—the more you can charge.

Your income is unlimited. If you become very successful and you do not have the time to take everyone's loan application, you can easily hire an assistant, or two, or more! You can then open your own company and have multiple offices in town, or in your state, or across the country.

Only you can say how much you will make. If you have the qualities needed to succeed, there will be nothing in your way. If you make the decision that this is what you want to do, and are determined to be a success, our company can help you with the rest.

The top mortgage brokers do over $100 million in loans a year. The average house in the country is worth $170,000. Divide 100 million by 170,000 and you get 588 loans. That's 2.45 loans each workday. If we estimate $1,500 average commission per loan, that equals $882,000 in gross income. (And please note, the average commission for top brokers is well over $1,500.)

But let's be conservative. Let's say you originate 1 loan a week. To be honest, this is a very low number. But we are being conservative, so let's play it out. If you take 2 weeks off every year, that means you originate 50 loans a year. Multiplied by $1,500 equals $75,000. Not bad, but it is on the low side.

Some of our students originate 20–30 loans per month and take several months off every year! And the only thing different about them is that they invest the time, effort, and the money needed to learn the marketing techniques to build their businesses to the point where they can set it on autopilot and let it run for them.

So far, we have been talking only about residential loans. You can just as easily get into commercial loans. Not only do commercial loans bring in a lot more money, but they are harder to do, so you can charge a lot more money because of that.

It is not uncommon to see a broker making 4–5% in loan fees on a million-dollar property. You can help finance anything: shopping centers, apartment buildings, churches, office complexes, etc.

My company is currently working on an e-class called "How To Jump Start Your Mortgage Career." It's a class for newcomers as well as veterans who need a little push. The class will cover all aspects of getting off to a great start by setting your goals and financial game plan, helping you understand the value of the numbers, teaching you the most effective marketing techniques, and how to get potential borrowers to commit to an application. For more info about these special classes, visit our website, **www.mortgagebrokertraining.com.**

CAN I WORK FROM HOME?

Most likely, yes. Many brokers have an office in their home. But you will have to report to your company's office every once in a while for meetings and to pick up your checks.

To set up a home office, you will need basic equipment: computer, fax, copy machine, mortgage software on the computer, and a phone.

Most companies actually prefer that you work from home. It results in fewer expenses for them. You can do almost everything from home that you can do in an office, except the paperwork. The processors will be handling the actual documents and you might have to be there to answer questions they may have. But that will not be too often.

If you do work at home, you will have to be more disciplined than most people are. It is easy to start goofing off and finding an excuse to stop working during the day. You'll have to remind yourself that, just because you work at home, it doesn't mean you can take off whenever you want to. Distractions are much more common at home than in the office. So if you do work at home, just get your work done first, and then take off all the time you want.

SO WHAT EXACTLY DOES A MORTGAGE BROKER DO?

The primary function of a mortgage broker is to generate loans, to convince people to get their mortgage from him. Once that is done, the broker can take the mortgage application and set the interest rate and program for the loan. After that, the broker can turn the paperwork over to the processor, who handles the rest. The broker will still have to stay involved and abreast of the loan as it progresses.

The borrowers place their trust in the broker, so whenever they have a question, they usually call him, not the processor.

In some companies there are no processors or the processors do very little. In that case, the broker must do all the paperwork himself. That includes: arranging for all verifications, locking the loan, ordering credit reports, appraisal, setting up pest inspections, getting the insurance, satisfying any conditions of the lender, and arranging the closing. If a broker is expected to do all this, he is entitled to a larger split as well as the processing fee.

The loan officer is the salesman of the company. Without loan officers, there would be no loans and no income. Marketing can get people into the door, but loan officers are needed to put the prospects at ease, help them understand the process, and convince them to make an application.

Mortgage brokers get loans. That's what they do. And that is what they get the big bucks for.

Large mortgage companies do a lot of image advertising, which means they advertise the company itself and not the individual loan officers. But in smaller companies, it is the loan officers people go to see. As a mortgage broker, your clients will look to you personally to get their loan done. And they will remember you. In fact, it is part of your job that they remember you more than they remember the company. That way, if you decide to go to another company, they will still get their next loan from you.

The following information is from the U.S. Department of Labor. It will give you another perspective of the role and duties of a mortgage broker.

Please keep in mind that the classification discussed below is "Loan Officer" in general. This includes bank loan officers, car loan officers and many others. The numbers given are for all loan officers, not just mortgage loan officers.

SIGNIFICANT POINTS

- Training or experience in banking, lending, or sales is advantageous.

- Slower than average employment growth for loan officers is expected because technology is making loan processing and approval simpler and faster.

- Earnings often fluctuate with the number of loans generated, rising substantially when the economy is good and interest rates are low.

NATURE OF THE WORK

For many individuals, taking out a loan may be the only way to afford a house, car, or college education. Likewise for businesses, loans are essential to start many companies, purchase inventory, or invest in capital equipment. Loan officers facilitate this lending by seeking potential clients and assisting them in applying for loans. Loan officers also gather information about clients and businesses to ensure that an informed decision is made regarding the quality of the loan and the probability of repayment.

Loan officers usually specialize in commercial, consumer, or mortgage loans. Commercial or business loans help companies pay for new equipment or expand operations; consumer loans include home equity, automobile, and personal loans; and mortgage loans are made to purchase real estate or to refinance an existing mortgage. As banks and other financial institutions begin to offer new types of loans and a growing variety of financial services, loan officers will have to keep abreast of these new product lines so that they can meet their customers' needs.

In many instances, loan officers act as salespeople. Commercial loan officers, for example, contact firms to determine their needs for loans. If a firm is seeking new funds, the loan officer will try to persuade the company to obtain the loan from their institution. Similarly, mortgage loan officers develop relationships with commercial and residential real estate agencies so that, when an individual or firm buys a property, the real estate agent might recommend contacting a specific loan officer for financing.

Once this initial contact has been made, loan officers guide clients through the process of applying for a loan. This process begins with a formal meeting or telephone call with a prospective client, during which the loan officer obtains basic information about the purpose of the loan and explains the different types of loans and credit terms that are available to the applicant. Loan officers answer questions about the process and sometimes assist clients in filling out the application.

After a client completes the application, the loan officer begins the process of analyzing and verifying the application to determine the client's creditworthiness. Often, loan officers can quickly access the client's credit history by computer and obtain a credit "score." This score represents the creditworthiness of a person or business as assigned by a software program that makes the evaluation. In cases where a credit history is not available or where unusual financial circumstances are present, the loan officer may request additional financial information from the client or, in the case of commercial loans, copies of the company's financial statements. With this information, loan officers who specialize in evaluating a client's creditworthiness—often called loan underwriters—may conduct a financial analysis or other risk assessment. Loan officers include this information and their written comments in a loan file, which is used to analyze whether the prospective loan meets the lending institution's requirements. Loan officers then decide, in consultation with their managers, whether to grant the loan. If the loan is approved, a repayment schedule is arranged with the client.

A loan may be approved that would otherwise be denied if the customer can provide the lender with appropriate collateral—property pledged as security for the repayment of a loan. For example, when lending money for a college education, a bank may insist that borrowers offer their home as collateral. If the borrowers were ever unable to repay the loans, the homes would be seized under court order and sold to raise the necessary money.

Loan counselors, also called loan collection officers, contact borrowers with delinquent loan accounts to help them find a method of repayment to avoid their defaulting on the loan. If a repayment plan cannot be developed, the loan counselor initiates collateral liquidation, in which the collateral used to secure the loan—a home or car, for example—is seized by the lender and sold to repay the loan. A loan officer may also perform this function.

WORKING CONDITIONS

Working as a loan officer usually involves considerable travel. For example, commercial and mortgage loan officers frequently work away from their offices and rely on laptop computers, cellular phones, and pagers to keep in contact with their offices and clients. Mortgage loan officers often work out of their homes or cars, visiting offices or homes of clients while completing loan applications. Commercial loan officers sometimes travel to other cities to prepare complex loan agreements.

Consumer loan officers and loan counselors, however, are likely to spend most of their time in an office.

Most loan officers and counselors work a standard 40-hour week, but many work longer, depending on the number of clients and the demand for loans. Mortgage loan officers can work especially long hours because they are free to take on as many customers as they choose. Loan officers usually carry a heavy caseload and sometimes cannot accept new clients until they complete current cases. They are especially busy when interest rates are low, a condition that triggers a surge in loan applications.

EMPLOYMENT

Loan officers and counselors held about 265,000 jobs in 2000. Approximately half were employed by commercial banks, savings institutions, and credit unions. Others were employed by nonbank financial institutions, such as mortgage banking and brokerage firms and personal credit firms.

Loan officers are employed throughout the U.S., but most work in urban and suburban areas. At some banks, particularly in rural areas, the branch or assistant manager often handles the loan application process.

TRAINING, OTHER QUALIFICATIONS, AND ADVANCEMENT

Loan officer positions generally require a bachelor's degree in finance, economics, or a related field. Most employers prefer applicants who are familiar with computers and their applications in banking. For commercial or mortgage loan officer jobs, training or experience in sales is highly valued by potential employers. Loan officers without college degrees usually have reached their positions by advancing through the ranks of an organization and acquiring several years of work experience in various other occupations, such as teller or customer service representative.

Various banking-related associations and private schools offer courses and programs for students interested in lending, as well as for experienced loan officers who want to keep their skills current. Completion of these courses and programs generally enhances one's employment and advancement opportunities.

A person planning a career as a loan officer or mortgage broker should be capable of developing effective working relationships with others, confident in his abilities, and highly motivated. For public relations purposes, loan officers must be willing to attend community events as representatives of their employer.

Capable loan officers and counselors may advance to larger branches of the firm or to managerial positions, while less capable workers—and those having inadequate academic preparation—could be assigned to smaller branches and might find promotion difficult. Advancement beyond a loan officer position usually includes supervising other loan officers and clerical staff.

JOB OUTLOOK

Automation of many financial services and the growing use of online mortgage brokers are expected to have a significant impact on the demand for lending professionals. However, population growth and the increasing variety of loans and other financial services that loan officers promote will ensure modest employment increases for these professionals.

Employment of loan officers is projected to increase more slowly than the average for all occupations through 2010. In contrast, loan counselors are expected to grow about as fast as the average for all occupations through 2010 as requirements for filing for bankruptcy tighten, forcing many to seek counseling to manage their debt. Most job openings will result from the need to replace workers who retire or otherwise leave the occupation permanently. As in the past, college graduates and those with banking, lending, or sales experience should have the best job prospects.

The use of credit scoring has made the loan evaluation process much simpler than in the past, and even unnecessary in some cases. Credit scoring allows loan officers, particularly loan underwriters, to evaluate many more loans in much less time, thus increasing loan officers' efficiency. In addition, the mortgage application process has become highly automated and standardized. This simplification has enabled online mortgage loan vendors to offer loan shopping services over the Internet. Online vendors accept loan applications from customers over the Internet and determine which lenders have the best interest rates for that particular loan. With this knowledge, customers can go directly to the lending institution, thereby bypassing mortgage loan brokers. Shopping for loans on the Internet—though currently not a widespread practice—is expected to become more common over the next 10 years, particularly for mortgages, thus reducing demand for loan officers.

Employment in banking generally is less affected by the upturns and downturns of the economy than is employment in other industries, contributing to job stability in banking occupations. Although loans remain a major source of revenue for banks, demand for new loans fluctuates and affects the income and employment opportunities of loan officers. When the economy is on the upswing or when interest rates decline dramatically, there is a surge in real estate buying and mortgage refinancing that requires loan officers to work long hours processing applications and induces lenders to hire additional loan officers.

Loan officers often are paid by commission on the value of the loans they place, and some have high earnings when demand for mortgages is high. When the real estate market slows, loan officers often suffer a decline in earnings and may even be subject to layoffs. The same applies to commercial loan officers, whose workloads increase during good economic times as companies seek to invest more in their businesses. In difficult economic conditions, loan counselors are likely to see an increase in the number of delinquent loans.

EARNINGS

Median annual earnings of loan counselors were $32,160 in 2000. The middle 50 percent earned between $25,290 and $43,510. The lowest 10 percent earned less than $20,850, while the top 10 percent earned more than $62,380.

Median annual earnings of loan officers were $41,420 in 2000. The middle 50 percent earned between $30,610 and $57,250. The lowest 10 percent earned less than $24,200, while the top 10 percent earned more than $82,640. Median annual earnings in the industries employing the largest numbers of loan officers in 2000 were:

Commercial banks $43,370

Savings institutions 42,760

Mortgage bankers and brokers 42,100

Personal credit institutions 35,040

Credit unions 29,700

The form of compensation for loan officers varies. Most loan officers are paid a commission that is based on the number of loans they originate. In this way, commissions are used to motivate loan officers to bring in more loans. Some institutions pay only salaries, while others pay their loan officers a salary plus a commission or bonus, based on the number of loans originated. Banks and other lenders sometimes offer their loan officers free checking privileges and somewhat lower interest rates on personal loans.

According to a salary survey conducted by Robert Half International, a staffing services firm specializing in accounting and finance, mortgage loan officers earned between $36,000 and $48,000 in 2000; consumer loan officers with 1 to 3 years of experience, between $42,250 and $56,750; and commercial loan officers with 1 to 3 years of experience, between $48,000 and $64,750. With over 3 years of experience, commercial loan officers could make between $66,000 and $95,250, and consumer loan officers can make between $55,500 and $75,500. Smaller banks ordinarily paid 15 percent less than larger banks.

Loan officers who are paid on a commission basis usually earn more than those on salary only.

CHAPTER 3

A Background of the Mortgage Industry

Mortgage brokers broker loans. They do not actually lend money themselves. That is why they need lenders.

A lender is any company or person that puts up the money and lets someone borrow it in order to pay for the house. The lender tells the broker what it wants in return (profit) and what expectations it has of the borrower (qualifications).

Once the loan is made and the house is bought, the loan is said to be part of the lender's loan portfolio. Some lenders have a very large portfolio and keep many of the loans they make.

The majority of lenders sell the loan to the secondary market in order to get their money back, so they can fund another loan to another borrower.

The secondary market is made up of very large, government-backed companies that keep the money flowing. A secondary market lender will buy hundreds of loans from any lender and bundle them together. Parts of this bundle will be sold to the investing public. These investments are called mortgage-backed securities.

By selling parts of the bundle, smaller investors can purchase an investment that has a set rate of return and that is backed by real estate as collateral. Also, the secondary market lender gets money back to go and buy more mortgages from primary lenders.

That is where the terms "conventional" and "conforming" come from. These terms refer to loans that fit the secondary market lender's strict criteria of loans it will purchase. If a loan is "conventional" or "conforming," any lender will fund it, because it will be easy to sell on the secondary market. It's almost guaranteed. And thus, the borrower will get the lowest rate possible, because his loan is very easy to do.

On the other hand, if a loan does not meet the secondary market lender's criteria, then it is said to be "non-conforming" or "sub-prime." There are still primary lenders that fund these loans, but they normally have to keep them in their own portfolio. And since they are smaller than the government-backed secondary lenders, they have to charge much higher interest to offset the risk.

Thus, non-conforming loans are harder for brokers to do because there are fewer lenders that fund them.

PRIMARY AND SECONDARY MARKETS

Lenders in the Primary Market are the best known. They are the companies borrowers use to get their loans. They advertise heavily and encourage borrowers to come to them to obtain their loans.

They usually process the loans based on Federal National Mortgage Association (FNMA) guidelines. If everything is kosher, they use their own money to fund the loan. As soon as closing has occurred, and sometimes even before closing, they look to sell the loan to an investor on the secondary market. This is where the really big players are. These investors buy trillions of dollars worth of loans a year. They usually repay the initial investor whatever they paid out, plus a premium for selling them the loan. The secondary investor is the new mortgage holder and can either service (collect payments) the loan itself or hire another company to do this for them.

The secondary lender then bundles together several hundred loans and sells bonds to the general public, which are secured by the interest these loans will bring. These bonds are known as mortgage-backed securities. By selling these bonds, the secondary investor raises more money to buy more loans and repeat the process.

THE PRIMARY MARKET IS COMPRISED OF THE FOLLOWING:

Savings and Loan Associations—S&Ls are specialized financial organizations that have traditionally been the largest source of residential mortgages.

Commercial Banks—Mortgages are extremely attractive to commercial bankers, especially if the borrower also happens to be a potential client with a personal account.

Life Insurance Companies—Many insurance companies do commercial mortgages on office buildings, shopping centers, and apartment complexes. There are some that deal directly with the public through mortgage brokers and mortgage bankers.

Credit Unions—Since 1978 federal regulators allowed credit unions to make mortgage loans with limitations on loan amounts. In 1982 these restrictions were lifted. Today almost 8,000 credit unions make first mortgages to their customers.

Mortgage Bankers—Institutions and individuals that create mortgages by using their own money and money from pension funds and insurance companies.

Mortgage Brokers—Institutions and individuals find and match investors with people who need money. A mortgage broker is a loan origination specialist, but not a lender.

Sellers—When interest rates are high, as they were in 1980 and 1981, when interest rates were 16 and 17 percent, many home sales involve seller financing. Also, many times, older sellers prefer to finance the sale of their home themselves to provide them with a stable monthly income.

SECONDARY LENDERS

Most people are familiar with primary lenders but they have no concept of secondary lenders, multi-billion-dollar organizations that play a key role in the mortgage financing system.

Suppose a local primary lender has $3 million available for mortgages. If the primary lender approves 20 loans of $150,000 each with loans terms of 15 and 30 years, it will run out of money to lend for a substantial amount of time. So to solve this problem, the primary lender sells its loans to the secondary lender to free up its cash.

FNMA, or Fannie Mae, was established by the government to help bring relief to these institutions by buying these loans from them so they can continue to loan fresh mortgage money to more homebuyers. FNMA buys conventional, Federal Housing Administration, and Department of Veterans Affairs loans as well as second trusts and adjustable-rate mortgages. This is a publicly held company and has mortgage-backed securities outstanding worth billions of dollars.

The Government National Mortgage Association (GNMA), or Ginnie Mae, is part of the Department of Housing and Urban Development (HUD). It assembles and guarantees pools of FHA and VA mortgages. Investors may participate in such pools by purchasing pass-through certificates on which they receive monthly payments for both interest and principal.

The Federal Home Loan Mortgage Corporation (FHLMC), or Freddie Mac, is a part of the Federal Home Loan Bank. Freddie Mac purchases Conventional, VA and FHA loans that meet its standards and finances such purchases through the sale of mortgage-backed bonds to the private sector. The federal government does not back Freddie Mac.

The Farmers Home Administration (FMHA) is a branch of the U.S. Department of Agriculture and provides low-interest home loans to low- and moderate-income families living in small towns or rural areas.

Apart from these four major secondary lenders, there are smaller private investors as well. These smaller lenders are more flexible in the types of loans they will buy and the qualifications of the borrowers. They mainly concentrate on non-conforming loans, which tend to be loans to riskier borrowers. These are called "sub-prime lenders."

Sub-prime lending is sometimes referred to as "predatory lending" by the media because of the higher rates involved. But without sub-prime mortgages, hundreds of thousands of people would be unable to own their homes.

It is true that the nature of sub-prime loans, along with the desperation of the borrowers, can lead mortgage brokers to get greedy and charge much more than they should.

The following is a press release about this growing problem from the U.S. Department of Housing and Urban Development (HUD):

HUD RELEASES NEW STUDY SHOWING EXPLOSION OF SUB-PRIME HOME LOANS IN BLACK AND LOW-INCOME NEIGHBORHOODS, AS CUOMO RAISES CONCERNS OF WIDESPREAD CONSUMER ABUSES BY PREDATORY LENDERS

Washington—Housing Secretary Andrew Cuomo today released a study showing that the number of sub-prime home loans is skyrocketing in predominantly black neighborhoods and low-income neighborhoods. While expanded access to credit is critical, there is growing evidence that some lenders may be engaged in predatory lending that is making home-ownership far more costly for blacks and poor families than for whites and middle-class families.

Cuomo released the study, *Unequal Burden: Income and Racial Disparities in Sub-prime Lending in America,* at the start of the meeting of a new Predatory Lending Task Force, and announced that Treasury Secretary Lawrence H. Summers will join him as co-chair of the Task Force.

Key findings of the Department of Housing and Urban Development analysis show that: 1) From 1993 to 1998, the number of sub-prime refinancing loans increased ten-fold. 2) Sub-prime loans are three times more likely in low-income neighborhoods than in high-income neighborhoods. 3) Sub-prime loans are five times more likely in black neighborhoods than in white neighborhoods. 4) Homeowners in high-income black areas are twice as likely as homeowners in low-income white areas to have sub-prime loans.

"This study documents shocking disparities, showing that too many African American and poor working families have sub-prime home loans, which may raise their costs of

homeownership," Secretary Cuomo said. "This raises concerns of widespread consumer fraud by predatory lenders.
HUD and Treasury are now examining these issues and
will report on this growing problem."

Secretary Summers said: "Greater access to capital, especially for those who traditionally have not had access to
capital, is crucial for American families and the American
economy. But it is essential that credit be provided in a
transparent and non-exploitative way. That is why we
will work on this Task Force to find ways of maximizing
credit access while avoiding predatory lending."

"We need legislation that will prohibit the secondary market, Government Sponsored Enterprises, from purchasing
predatory loans," Cuomo added. "We should define by legislation what is a predatory loan and the terms and conditions. This should not be a matter of Government Sponsored
Enterprises discretion."

The HUD study focused primarily on home refinancing
loans, which account for 80 percent of sub-prime loans. Sub-
prime lending involves providing credit to borrowers with past
credit problems, who cannot qualify for the conventional prime

market. Sub-prime lending can include predatory lending, which hits homebuyers with excessive mortgage fees, interest rates, penalties and pre-paid credit life insurance charges that can raise the cost of home buying by thousands of dollars for individual families.

DETAILS OF STUDY FINDINGS

The study found that from 1993 to 1998: The number of sub-prime home refinancing loans increased tenfold to more than 790,000. In 1993, the sub-prime share of the overall mortgage market represented $20 billion. In 5 years, this volume multiplied more than seven times to $150 billion.

Sub-prime loans accounted for 51 percent of home loan refinancing in predominantly African American neighborhoods in 1998—but only 9 percent in white neighborhoods. Comparable 1993 figures were 8 percent in black neighborhoods and 1 percent in white neighborhoods.

The racial disparity is so wide that 39 percent of families in high-income black neighborhoods received sub-prime home loans in 1998, while less than half that number of families in low-income white neighborhoods received sub-prime loans.

In low-income neighborhoods, sub-prime loans accounted for 26 percent of total loans in 1998—compared with only 11 percent in moderate-income neighborhoods and just 7 percent in upper-income neighborhoods. Comparable 1993 figures were 3 percent in low-income neighborhoods and 1 percent each in moderate-income and upper-income neighborhoods.

The analysis points out that by providing loans to borrowers who do not meet the credit standards for borrowers in the prime market, sub-prime lending serves a critical role in the nation's economy. These borrowers may have blemishes on their credit records, insufficient credit history or non-traditional credit sources. Through the sub-prime loan market, they can buy a new home, improve their existing home, or refinance their mortgage to increase their cash on hand.

The study adds that prime lenders have made significant efforts and progress in reaching historically underserved markets and communities. However, based on the explosive growth of sub-prime lending in these neighborhoods, much remains to be done, in both the primary and secondary markets.

The HUD analysis is the first look at the most recent nationwide data on sub-prime lending broken down by the income and racial characteristics of neighborhoods nationwide. It is based on a study of nearly 1 million home loans.

CHAPTER 4

Choosing a Company to Work For

HOW DO I DECIDE WHAT COMPANY TO WORK FOR?

If you are not going to open your own company right away, you will need to work for another company to get some experience. And, depending on your state laws, you might have to get some experience before you are allowed to open your own company.

First, your best bet is to choose a company that has a large presence in your area and does its own marketing to bring in borrowers. Many companies do very little company-sponsored marketing and expect their brokers to get their own loans by doing their own marketing.

Secondly, look for one that offers a training program. These companies are few, but when you start, training is essential.

There are many things that could go wrong with a loan. The more you know, the better off you are. Plus, you will instill more confidence in your borrowers when you can confidently answer their questions.

If you prefer to get training elsewhere, you can try your local real estate school, community college, and, of course, you can visit **www.mortgagebrokertraining.com** to obtain the best-selling training manual in the industry, *Residential Mortgage Loan Origination Made Easy.*

Thirdly, it should be easy for you to make money. The commission split should be at least at 50%. There should be no monthly fees. And training should not cost you anything, either.

Most companies are always looking for new brokers. Others do not want new brokers. The best way to find a company to work for is to search the want ads to see who is looking.

Once you get into the business, you will get a feel for the market and learn about opportunities at other companies. The companies that hire the most also lose the most people, and are mainly interested in churning out loans. This same thing happens in the real estate industry. According to popular belief, everyone has at least a couple of loans in them. Once they get into the business, they tell all their relatives and friends. These relatives and friends then let this person do their loans. After the new broker runs out of friends and relatives that need a loan, they stop earning money, and eventually quit to find another job. So the company hires as many people as it can in order to get to those friends and relatives.

If you take this profession seriously and do the right things from the beginning, this will not happen to you.

Once you get some experience and develop a track record of success, you will be able to walk into any mortgage company and get a job. As you do more loans, your commission split should also increase. If it does not, look for another place or start your own company.

Once you can demonstrate that you can originate a large number of loans, you should be offered a salary in addition to your commission. What you negotiate with your boss is up to you. But if you are making the company money, they will want to keep you and should increase your compensation.

The new trend in the industry is to offer brokers 100% commission. Every company has its own guidelines, but under this plan, you keep the entire Origination Fee and any YSP. The company gets a set fee per loan and also a desk fee per month. These companies offer almost no training, so it might not be a good idea to start at one of these places, but once you get going, you might consider it. It is almost the same as opening your own company, but without the overhead.

Check the Internet job boards for any openings in your area. Websites like **www.monster.com** list hundreds of jobs available in the real estate financing industry.

IS MY JOB SECURE?

Very secure. A job as a mortgage broker is the most secure job you can have—especially since you work on commission. If you do not produce, they do not have to pay you. You also do not eat, so it is a good idea to produce as much as you can. Your job relies entirely on your willingness to work. Your job security will always be totally in your own hands.

Mortgage companies come and go. The one you work for might fail and go out of business. It doesn't matter. There are a thousand others that will love to hire you. The key is production. If you produce loans, you will have people throwing incentives at you to get you to work for them.

You never have to worry about being laid off again. And if you set your business up the right way, you do not have to worry about the ups and downs of the economy. People will always have to move, buy, and sell their houses. And in today's easy finance society, no one pays cash for homes anymore. So every time someone sells a house, there is need for a mortgage.

CAN I DO THIS PART-TIME?

Sure. In fact, if you already have a stable job that earns you a good income you should probably start off part-time first. See how you like the business. Once you start making enough, you can make the jump into full-time. That's how most people do it anyway. Any time you start a new job it is a risk. And in this case, there is no stable paycheck to rely on.

So common sense dictates that you either start part-time until you are making enough in commissions to support yourself and your family, or you have enough in the bank to support you for a few months until you start earning.

There are many brokers who started out part-time and then graduated to full-time status. And there is not much that cannot be done at night or on the weekends. The processing will be done by the processors in your office.

One of the reasons that brokers actually go to peoples' homes to get applications signed is because they are part-time.

If you are full-time, you would want the borrowers to come to your office. Psychologically, it works in your favor. But if you cannot do that, meet wherever you have to, to get the loan.

Keep in mind that borrowers will not like it if they find out that you are not full-time. Since buying a house is a big deal to most people, they would rather have an experienced professional. That's just human nature. So be sure that you do not volunteer the fact that you are part-time.

Another thing to keep in mind is, loans take a long time to close. And you do not get paid until they close. The average loan takes up to 30 days to close. Once you take the application, you still have to wait another month until you see any money. You need to have enough loans closing so that if you do not get paid for 2–3 weeks you will still be OK.

CHAPTER 5

Opening Your Own Company

Once you get the hang of the business and start producing several loans a month, you might decide to open your own company.

Borrowers like it even more when they know they are dealing with the owner of the company and not just an employee.

Starting your own company is not as hard as it sounds, either. You will already know how to get loans, and you should have a good idea how to process them, or you can hire a processor. The hardest part is finding lenders, but if you have been in the business, you will meet and get to know the lender representatives, and they will be happy to help you get approved with them once you go out on your own.

Another way to find lenders is by looking through mortgage magazines, like the ones mentioned in this book. They all have ads from lenders looking for brokers. Or you can check out the websites of the NAMB and your state association. They will most likely have ads of lenders, and many lenders will be members.

The overhead can be minimal. Rent and employees will be your largest expenses. You will also need to spend money for advertising, but you were probably doing that working for someone else anyway.

The biggest reward is not having to split the commission. Going from a 50% commission split to owning to keeping 100% because it's your own company is like doing twice as many loans.

How soon you can open your own company depends on your state regulations. Some states let you open right away. Others require you to work in the industry for a certain amount of time before you can open your own.

One concept that has been catching on lately is "net branching." This is where a lender wants to open offices, but does not want to spend the money, so it lets you open an office for them.

You become an employee of the lender, and manage your office. You are allowed to run it any way you want, and your compensation is based on the net profits of the office. It lets you use its corporate name and all its lenders or it can fund your loans itself.

As net branching became popular, companies started calling themselves: net branches, branch affiliates, virtual loan originators, interactive partners, partner branches, affiliate branching, and retail branch networks. They all pretty much mean the same thing.

Net branching is one step away from working for someone else and one step away from owning your own company. It's right in the middle of both.

The one downside of opening your own company is that it is hard to get approved to do FHA and VA loans. You have to go through a strict approval process with both agencies. And the requirements are strict. Many smaller mortgage brokers do not bother, and only do conventional and sub-prime loans.

But if you choose net branching, you can do both FHA and VA from Day 1 if the company is already approved, and it should be.

Some other benefits of net branching include:

- The ability to close loans as a broker or a banker.

- No state requirements to meet to open an office.

- Fewer disclosures to give to borrowers.

- If you close a loan as a broker, the customer will know how much the broker makes for the YSP.

- The company provides accounting and payroll services.

- Group benefits.

- Legal and compliance support.

- Marketing help.

- Computer and technology help.

Some of the disadvantages are:

- The lender gets a portion of the commission on each loan.

- You are an employee and have to go by the lender's guidelines—including hiring and firing personnel.

- If the company fails, you have nothing.

- If you choose the wrong net branch, and want to cancel the agreement, you have to start over with a new company name and expenses.

- Most of the good ones require you to have experience and production before they will work with you.

CHAPTER 6

How Do I Get Started?

BASIC REQUIREMENTS

The requirements vary from state to state, but they are generally the same.

You must be at least 18 years old and able to enter into contracts, so you must be of sound mind. Also, if your state has licensing, you will have to be fingerprinted and your background will be checked before a license will be issued.

In some states, you will need to pass an exam before you get your license. They want to be sure you have some idea of what you are doing before you start.

In most states, you will have to take a class, which may have a test at the end that you will be required to pass. These classes are more like driving school than the SAT, so even if you sleep through the whole thing, you probably will still pass.

WHAT DO I DO FIRST?

The first thing you do is some homework. Don't make a face, it's not hard. Get on your computer and do a search for your state's banking department.

Look for any reference to mortgage licenses. Or you can just do a search for "(your state) mortgage license" Through these searches you will find the website that will provide the most up-to-date and detailed instructions on exactly what you need to do.

As of the date this is being written, 45 states have laws requiring mortgage broker licenses, but most do not require that individuals have licenses. Only companies are required to have a license. Texas and Florida are the two largest that require everyone working in the business to have a license.

More states will follow these two.

Check below for your state:

Alabama
www.bank.state.al.us

Alaska
www.dced.state.ak.us/bsc/mortgagelender.htm

Arkansas
www.accessarkansas.org

Arizona
www.azbanking.com

California
www.dre.cahwnet.gov

Colorado
www.ago.state.co.us

Connecticut
www.state.ct.us/dob/pages/1stmtg.htm

Delaware
www.state.de.us/bank/applyfor.htm
www.state.de.us/bank/mbintro.htm

District of Columbia
www.obfi.washingtondc.gov/services/mortgage_app.shtm

Florida
www.dbf.state.fl.us/licensing/MBlist.html

Georgia
www.ganet.org.dbf
www.ganet.org/cgibin/pub/ocode/
    ocgsearch?docname=OCode/G/7/3/5&highlight=7-3-5

Hawaii
www.state.hi.us/dcca/
www.capitol.hawaii.gov/hrscurrent/
    Vol10/hrs454/HRS_454-3.htm

Idaho
www2.state.id.us/finance/dof.htm

Indiana
www.in.gov/pla/
www.inamb.com/education.asp

Illinois
www.obre.state.il.us/
www.obre.state.il.us/RESFIN/mortbank.htm

Iowa
www.idob.state.ia.us/

Kansas
www.osbckansas.org/DOCML/docmllawsandregs.html

Kentucky
www.dfi.state.ky.us/
http://162.114.4.13/KRS/288-00/CHAPTER.HTM

Louisiana
www.ofi.state.la.us/
www.ofi.state.la.us/lcclidx.htm

Maine
www.state.me.us/pfr/ccp/ccphome2.htm
http://janus.state.me.us/legis/statutes/9-A/
 title9-Ach00sec0.html

Maryland
www.dllr.state.md.us/license/fin_reg/mortlend/mdfinreg.html
http://mlis.state.md.us/cgi-win/web_statutes.exe

Massachusetts
www.state.ma.us/dob/

Michigan
www.cis.state.mi.us/fis/ind_srch/mortgage/
 mortgage_industry_criteria.asp

Minnesota
www.commerce.state.mn.us/mainfe.htm
www.revisor.leg.state.mn.us/stats/58/

Mississippi
www.dbcf.state.ms.us/
www.dbcf.state.ms.us/slregs98sept.htm

Missouri
www.ecodev.state.mo.us/finance/
www.moga.state.mo.us/STATUTES/C367.HTM

Montana
www.commerce.state.mt.us/Bnk&Fin/index.html

Nebraska
www.ndbf.org/fin.htm
www.ndbf.org/mb-act.pdf

Nevada
www.fid.state.nv.us/
www.leg.state.nv.us/NRS/NRS-645B.html

New Hampshire
www.state.nh.us/banking

New Jersey
www.naic.org/nj/bank_div.htm
www.njleg.state.nj.us/cgi-bin/...

New Mexico
www.rld.state.nm.us/fid/index.htm
www.rld.state.nm.us/fid/laws/otherregs.htm

New York
www.banking.state.ny.us
http://assembly.state.ny.us/leg/?cl=9

North Carolina
www.banking.state.nc.us/
www.banking.state.nc.us/gs/gs53a15.htm

North Dakota
www.state.nd.us/bank/
http://ranch.state.nd.us/LR/cencode/CCT47.pdf

Ohio
www.com.state.oh.us/ODOC/dfi/

Oklahoma
www.okdocc.state.ok.us
www.okdocc.state.ok.us/introMB.htm

Oregon
www.cbs.state.or.us/external/dfcs/mortgage/mortmain.htm

Pennsylvania
www.banking.state.pa.us/
www.banking.state.pa.us/PA_Exec/Banking/resource/acts.htm

Rhode Island
www.state.ri.us/manual/data/queries/stdept_.idc?id=100
www.rilin.state.ri.us/Statutes/TITLE19/19-14-2/INDEX.HTM

South Carolina
www.state.sc.us/consumer/

South Dakota
www.state.sd.us/dcr/bank/BANK-HOM.htm
http://legis.state.sd.us/statutes/Index.cfm

Tennessee
www.state.tn.us/financialinst/
www.state.tn.us/sos/rules/0180/0180.htm

Texas
www.tsld.state.tx.us/
www.tsld.state.tx.us/adoptedrules.htm

Utah
www.commerce.state.ut.us/re/
www.commerce.state.ut.us/re/mortgage/mortregfaq.htm

Vermont
www.bishca.state.vt.us
www.bishca.state.vt.us/BankingDiv/lenderapplic/PROCED.PDF

Virginia
www.state.va.us/scc/division/banking/index.htm

Washington
www.wa.gov/dfi/cs/mb.htm
www.wa.gov/dfi/cs/rcw19146.htm

West Virginia
www.wvdob.org/professionals/n_mortgage.htm

Wisconsin
www.wdfi.org/fi/mortbank/
www.wdfi.org/fi/mortbank/mbfaqs.htm#2

Wyoming
http://audit.state.wy.us/banking/

Another way to check is to visit **www.namb.org.** This is the website of the National Association of Mortgage Brokers. It also lists the states that need licenses and each state's licensing website. You can also visit the following site for this info: **http://www.thomas-law.com/mtgbrokers.html**

Your second step is to get your own license if you need to. Take a class if you have to. Most real estate schools offer mortgage classes. You can also go to your local community college. They almost always offer classes in real estate.

Your state might have you take a competency test. Pass with a certain percentage and you get your license, but if you don't pass, don't worry. Study harder and try again, and keep taking the test until you do pass.

If your state has individual licenses, mortgage classes and tests can cost you about $500.

Third, get a job. In Texas, you have to find a company to sponsor you before you can take the state test. So after you pass, you would work for this company. Elsewhere, you can look for a job while you are preparing for the state test, or as soon as you decide to become a mortgage broker. Getting a job and finding a company to work for has been discussed in another section.

Fourth, get an understanding of the job. Get all the forms and familiarize yourself with them. Get a copy of *Residential Mortgage Loan Origination Made Easy* from our website. Learn your company's policies and procedures. Take any training classes your company offers. And once you become a member of your local Association of Mortgage Brokers, you can take its training classes as well.

That's about it. The hardest part is deciding to take the plunge. Once you decide to become a mortgage broker, the rest is easy.

HOW LONG DOES IT TAKE TO START?

It depends on your state's laws. If you have to get your own license it could take up to 3 months. If not, you can be in the business in one day.

WHAT DO I HAVE TO KNOW?

Actually, nothing. You will learn everything you need as you go along. If you already have knowledge of the process, it will help you shorten the learning curve. If not, resources like this book will help you become a pro in no time.

Make sure you thoroughly understand the concepts discussed in this book. Pay attention to:

- What brokers do

- How they get paid

- The loan process

- The requirements to become a broker

After you decide that you want to become a broker, follow the steps outlined in this chapter. Then, after you become a broker, that's when the fun starts.

Marketing and loan origination are the two things you will be focused on. Getting people to come to you, trust you, and let you do their loans is what this business is all about.

CHAPTER 7

Would You Make A Good Broker?

TAKE THIS TEST TO SEE

The following test is designed to get you to think about your likes and dislikes, to see if you are a good candidate to be a mortgage broker.

1. Do you want to be your own boss?

2. Would you rather skip the morning rush-hour commute to a job every morning?

3. Are you willing to work on weekends?

4. Do you like working with people?

5. Can you use a calculator and basic software programs?

6. Will you be OK mentally with not earning a steady paycheck?

7. Can you discipline yourself to work a set schedule, even though no one is watching?

8. Can you budget your income?

9. Can you work nights in the beginning?

10. Can you handle rejection?

11. Are you willing to constantly keep learning?

12. Are you willing to spend money on your education?

13. Will you be comfortable asking people you know for business?

14. Can you stay focused and determined so you can withstand the ups and downs of the business?

15. Will you stick with it, even when the going gets a little rough?

16. Do you want to be a white-collar worker?

17. Are you an ethical person?

18. Can you be trusted with people's confidential and private information?

19. Do you work well with others?

20. When given responsibility, do you give it 100% effort?

21. Do you know a large number of people you can approach for business?

22. Have you ever studied marketing?

23. Are you willing to learn how to do marketing?

24. Are you willing to learn how to be a great salesperson?

25. Does the thought of earning what you are worth excite you?

These are the qualities you need to be a good mortgage broker. The more "Yes" answers you gave, the better.

Being a mortgage broker brings a lot of responsibility. Your actions can cause a lot of good or a lot of harm to your clients. Before you enter this business, make sure this is what you really want to do. Just like any other job, you will have to work hard to earn a living, but the rewards are great.

CHAPTER 8

The Loan Process

The loan process becomes child's play after you go through it a few times. But for the borrowers, it can be a daunting challenge.

It all starts with a rate quote. Generally, a potential borrower will tell you he is looking for a loan and ask what your rates are. A more sophisticated borrower will ask you for a Good Faith Estimate of your rate and all your fees.

In order to provide this information, you will have to know what type of loan he wants and what his credit looks like. Only then can you start quoting rates.

But let's say the guy likes whatever you told him and wants to move forward. The next step is to fill out the loan application, also known as the 1003. You will also gather any needed information to help him qualify. (Our company also requires a check for the appraisal and credit report at this time.)

Once you have all this, you turn it over to the processor, who starts working her magic. She puts the loan package together. She orders the appraisal and credit reports. She locks the loan in case you didn't already. She makes all the necessary copies and forwards them to the lender.

At the lender's, it takes the file a few days to get through underwriting. Once it does, the underwriter faxes a conditions sheet back to the processor. Most items will be OK, but there are a couple of documents still needed, so the processor calls the borrower to obtain these extra documents. She then forwards them to the underwriter, who then agrees to fund the loan.

The processor then calls the title company to open title and arrange for closing. Once the money is wired from the lender to the title company, closing can take place. In the meantime, the borrower has to show proof that he obtained homeowner's insurance on the house.

If everything is OK and the title is clear, the closing can take place, usually at the title company's office. All the documents are signed by the borrower and the loan is closed.

The title company will mail or courier your fees to your office and your office will write your check for your commission.

WHAT EXACTLY DOES THE PROCESSOR DO?

Most mortgage companies have processors. These people do the paperwork on the loan. The mortgage broker's main role is the get the loan and get the borrowers to agree to it. The processor then takes over and processes all the information, making it presentable to the lender.

The processor enters the 1003 and disclosures into the computer. She locks the loan; orders the appraisal and credit report; gathers all verifications; asks for any other needed info from the borrowers; satisfies any conditions of the lender; orders title and survey; and then arranges the closing.

But if you're smart, you won't just turn the file over to the processor and disappear. If the processor needs information from the borrowers, either she can get it or you can. It is better if you do it. They know you and trust you. In their minds, it will appear that you are involved in all aspects of their loan, and that is exactly how you want it to seem. Whatever the processor needs, get it to her right away. Take an active interest in your loans. It's surprising, but many brokers lose interest after they turn the file over to processing. They only help out when the loan is in trouble. (It wouldn't be in trouble if they'd stayed involved!) You worked so hard to get the loan, don't let anyone else drop the ball on your commission.

WHAT DOES AN UNDERWRITER DO?

The underwriter works for the lender. Once the paperwork is processed and the file is sent to the lender, the underwriter takes over and makes sure all the information is there so she can approve the loan. If something is missing or she needs more verifications, she will make those conditions of the loan. Until you supply her with the needed info, the loan will not be approved.

Some brokers see the underwriter as the enemy. Sometimes you will, too. But underwriters are people just like you and me. Their main objective is to keep their job. The truth is, they do not have much interest in your loan. They would just like it to close, so they can get a bonus. But if it doesn't close, they will still get their paycheck. So don't get mad at the underwriter.

Instead, make underwriters your friend. They get yelled at enough by other brokers. If you show them some kindness, they will return the favor by getting your loans through underwriting faster.

The process of underwriting is sometimes the longest part of the loan. Lenders try to get loans through underwriting in 2–3 business days. But when they are very busy, it can take over 9. So if your lock is about the expire and your loan is sitting in underwriting, it is in your best interest to be on good terms with the underwriters, who can push your file to the head of the line and save your commission in the process.

WHAT IS AN APPRAISER?

The appraiser tells you the value of the property. Almost all loans need an appraisal. The appraiser is also someone you should be good friends with, since he is the one who determines how much your borrowers can borrow.

The appraisal is an art, not a science. Send 10 appraisers to the same house and all of them will give you different values. They might be in the same ballpark, but they will all be different.

So if you find a "liberal" appraiser, be sure to keep him happy. For example, you are doing a refinance for a couple who need to take out $20,000 of equity from their house or they won't do the loan. Their balance is $50,000 and your lender will only lend up to 80% of the value. Closing costs can be assumed to be $4,000. The appraisal comes in at $90,000.

You have a problem, because you need the house to be worth $92,500 in order for the borrower to get 20K out. If you are on good terms with your appraiser, you can suggest that you need a value of at least $92,500. And if he likes you, he will do his best to justify an appraisal of $92,500.

WHERE DO I GET THE CREDIT REPORTS?

Your company should have an account set up with a local credit reseller. You get all your credit reports from this company, and you can usually do it by computer. No need to talk to anyone or fax anything. Just enter in the data of the borrowers, and their credit report will print on your printer.

Understanding the report will come with time, and you can find out exactly how to do so in *Residential Loan Origination Made Easy*. (Ordering info is available at the back of the book.)

The most important thing to notice is the credit score. The higher the score, the better the credit and the better the chances of the borrower getting a loan. If the score is 620 or above, it qualifies as a conforming loan. Under 620 makes it sub-prime.

To learn how easy it is to raise someone's credit scores read the book *How To Make Your Credit Sparkle,* which is also available at our website, **http://www.creditsparkle.com.**

WHAT DOES THE TITLE COMPANY DO?

The title company does many things, but its primary role is to make sure that the title on the house is clear. This means that no one besides the seller is claiming ownership of the property. If everything is OK, they will issue title insurance, which protects the buyer in case there is ever any problem with the title in the future.

Without clear title, the lender will not lend the money and the loan will not close. The title company also works as an escrow company and keeps all the funds until closing. When all the paperwork is complete, the lender wires the money into the title company's account. The title company will then prepare all the closing documents, get everyone's signatures and distribute all the checks.

A real estate closing attorney can also serve the same function as a title company. It really depends in which state you live in if you use title companies or escrow companies, or closing attorneys.

The fees charged by the title company are passed on to the buyers and sellers. In the sales contract, it specifies who will pay for the title charges.

CHAPTER 9

How Do People Choose Their Broker?

Over 65% of Americans use mortgage brokers. Brokers provide consumers with:

- Choice

- Convenience

- Expertise

The consumer receives an expert mentor through the complex mortgage-lending process. The broker offers the consumer extensive choices and access to affordable home loans while balancing the consumer's financial interests and goals.

So the question really is, "Why wouldn't someone use a mortgage broker?"

WHAT ABOUT THE COMPETITION?

There are a ton of mortgage companies in every city. They seem to be everywhere, so I can't say that there is not a lot of competition. There is. But it doesn't matter. You could not do all the loans in your town by yourself, anyway. There is enough business to go around. Over $2 trillion in loans are originated every year. That is a lot of money.

If you provide good customer service, are knowledgeable about your loan products, and take the time to care about your prospects and their needs, you will have more business than you can handle.

The National Association of Realtors does yearly surveys of homebuyers, and some of the results are listed below. These are for the 2003 survey.

91% of all homebuyers obtained a mortgage for their home purchase.

Why do they choose their mortgage lender? These were their reasons:

14% price
16% reputation
14% they had used the lender before
36% the lender was recommended by their agent
13% the lender recommended by family or friends.

Only 56% of homebuyers would definitely use their mortgage lender again. That shows that almost half the mortgage companies are not doing their job properly. This is very good news for those companies that really do a great job of customer satisfaction.

On average, homebuyers had a loan-to-value ratio of 84%. That means that on average people got loans of 84% of the value of the house.

48% of all buyers went to only one mortgage company.

When did they get a pre-approval?

38%   before looking for a house

30%   while searching for a house

28%   after they found a house

5%   never. They were not pre-approved.

Where did buyers find out about lenders?

41%   from their agent

32%   from the Internet

28%   from friends/family

26%   from going to different lenders

20%   from newspapers

16%   from telephone

6%   from direct mail

5%   from TV commercials.

So what do these numbers tell us?

1. Referrals are very important. Referrals from Realtors, friends, and family make up a large percentage of the reason why people choose a mortgage company.

2. Since a large number of people visit only one mortgage company, the risk of competition is not as high as one would think.

3. Price is not that big a deal when choosing a lender.

4. Traditional advertising (radio, TV, newspaper) is not as effective as word-of-mouth advertising, and it is a lot more expensive!

CHAPTER 10

The Keys to Success as a Mortgage Broker

Charles Schwab once said, "A man, to carry on a successful business, must have imagination. He must see things as in a vision, a dream of the whole thing." His words are true for both men and women who want to start in the mortgage brokerage business. Imagination is a major requirement.

WHAT WILL YOU NEED TO BE A SUCCESSFUL MORTGAGE BROKER?

Certainly you'll need your own special knowledge, skills, talent, some money, and a lot of time. But just as necessary is a personal desire to help others. This is important if you are an employee and is vital if you are an owner.

As a consumer, you can easily read the attitude of people who serve you. You know when someone is helping you because it is his job or because he enjoys doing his job. And clients usually respond by supporting and recommending those who help them solve their problems and make them feel important. They appreciate our business, and they get it.

Before you decide whether mortgage brokerage is for you, you must know who you are. What do you feel most comfortable doing? Under what conditions do you enjoy working with people? Under what conditions do you prefer to avoid people? What are your personal goals? What are your financial goals? How much risk do you feel comfortable taking? Most important, is financing a good fit in your life or would it cause more problems than it cures? Self-analysis can be difficult, but it is the only way of ensuring that this is what will bring you the results you want in life.

Maybe by this stage in your life you've developed a list of personal goals for the next year, five years, and beyond. Most people have not. It is not mandatory that you develop a long list of your life goals before you start in this business, but it will increase your chances of personal and financial success. You can begin by answering these questions for yourself:

- What is it you want from your life?

- Do you have specific goals?

- What plans do you have for the next year of your life?

- Is there anything that people often compliment you about?

- Is there some work or task you would do even if you were not paid?

- Is there some opportunity that strikes you as worthwhile?

PERSONAL VALUES

Values are tools that will take you toward your personal goals. Values are standards and qualities that you have established to help you make daily decisions. Those people who succeed in business have some common personal knowledge. Let's look at those values together to determine your strength in opportunities.

Self-awareness. The process of starting and operating a business is difficult. It will work if you constantly test yourself, maintaining what works and changing what doesn't. But that's what many people love about being a business owner, the endless challenges. It makes them aware of their characteristics and requires that they continue to grow.

Hard work. Being an independent businessman means that you get to select which 12 hours of the day you are going to work. Just kidding. But don't expect to work just a 40-hour week at least at first and you won't be disappointed.

Discipline. Discipline is the power behind hard work. You can know exactly what needs to be done and still not do it. Self-discipline forces you to act. Having goals that are meaningful to you will increase your self-discipline.

Independence. Great business owners often make poor employees. They are too independent. They cannot, however, be stubborn. Business owners must maintain a balance between independence and open-mindedness to succeed.

Self-confidence. It takes a lot of nerve to start a business. It takes a lot more to make it successful. But nerve or self-confidence is not equal. It is a belief in your unique skills founded on past success. You know you can successfully operate as a mortgage broker because you have the skills to do so, not just the desire.

Adaptability. Life is chaos. No matter how much we plan, people and events change. Products change. Markets change. We change. A successful business owner must adapt to these changes. It's a hassle sometimes. But remember, without change, life becomes very dull.

Judgment. To succeed in business, you must make good decisions every day. Wisdom requires knowledge. You must be able to gather complete and accurate facts in order to make the best decision you can from those facts. You will not be right every time, but you will be right most of the time. This is good judgment.

Stress tolerance. Stress has been defined as "the confusion created when your mind overrides your body's basic desire to club someone who desperately deserves it." Humor can help reduce stress. Stress is a part of every day life, especially in business. Learning to live with stress without taking it personally can help you succeed in business.

Need to achieve. Success is the achievement of something you set out to do. It may be the completion of a project, or the start of a business, or the learning of a new skill. This need is a driving force within successful business owners that helps give them the energy to reach their goal.

ABOUT YOUR FINANCIAL GOALS

As much as you may love helping people, you must also have financial goals. Without a fair salary and profit, you won't be able to help people get a loan.

What is an appropriate financial goal for you? If your business goal is to open your own office within 3 years, your financial goal must be one that will fund such an ambitious goal. If your business takes off and is successful, and you want to then sell it in 10 years and retire, your financial goals must match what you expect your selling price of your business will be. If your business goal is to make a salary as well as a fair return on your investment, you must first determine what a good salary and return are to you.

One successful mortgage broker established a financial goal of developing annual sales of $200,000 within 3 years in order to take on a partner who could offer other financial services. He then wanted to spend 2 more years developing the single location before selling the business to the partner for enough to pay off his home mortgage and do some traveling. His goals were specific and attainable.

YOUR RISK TOLERANCE

Business is legalized gambling. When you start any business you're gambling that you'll succeed. How much does this risk bother you? Are you risk tolerant?

You must determine your own risk tolerance and that of those with whom you share your life. If you're ready to take the plunge, but your spouse would rather not, find a mutually acceptable level of risk before starting your business. Or else you may find, as many people have, that you traded an invaluable relationship for a replaceable business.

GENERATING BUSINESS

Mortgage brokerage is a people business. The more people you know, the more loans you have the opportunity to do. It has been estimated that each person alive knows about 1,000 other people. Sounds like a large number, but it has been scientifically studied.

Out of all the people you know, I am sure there are many that you wouldn't want to work with, and some that wouldn't work with you, for whatever reason.

So the average person's sphere of influence (the group of known people you can market to) is much less than 1,000. It's closer to about 300. Given that at least 10% of the population moves every year, that gives the average mortgage broker a shot at 30 loans a year without doing any other marketing.

But in the beginning you will not have such a large sphere of influence. So while you build your own, you can use other people's spheres. There are many other professionals who also use the sphere of influence marketing concept: Realtors, insurance agents, financial planners, and anyone else who has a customer list.

The easiest way to increase your sales and your sphere is to convince one of these business owners to sell you to his customers. He can write a testimonial saying how wonderful you are and then mail it to his customers.

Or you can just get their names, or even pay for the names and addresses. Big companies do this all the time. You might not believe this, but there are lists available on any topic you could think of. For example, you can get a list of subscribers for every magazine in the country. You can get a list of people who buy Dean Martin videos. You can get a list of people who own houses worth over $1 million, with no mortgage and who own another house in Hawaii. The lists are endless.

My point is, while you should do your best to build your own list, you can in the meantime use someone else's to market to. And if you can get the list owner to recommend you, your marketing will be a lot more effective.

Let me prove it to you. Now that you have bought this book, you are on my list. Let's say that one day, you get two letters in the mail. One is from me saying that Joe's Mortgage Licensing School is the best school I have seen and that you should check it out. The other letter is from a company called Mary's Licensing School saying how good it is.

Which one sounds better? If you have enjoyed this book and feel that I know what I am talking about, then you will probably choose Joe's school.

This is the power of the endorsement. I endorsed Joe's school and my endorsement to my own list will carry a lot of weight, especially since my list already knows and trusts me.

The same is true for you. As people begin to know your work and trust you, you will come to know the same power of endorsement.

HOW DO I GET CLIENTS?

There are a zillion different ways to get customers and clients. In fact, my company has several different manuals and systems that show brokers how to get customers.

You can:

- go after the home buyer market

- go after the refinance market

- go after the people about to be foreclosed on market

- broker loans for investors

- broker loans for businesses

- factor account receivables

- buy and sell notes and mortgages

- do second mortgages

- focus on apartment complexes or shopping centers

- do construction loans

- do church financing

- do home equity loans

- do FHA or VA loans

- do sub-prime loans

- do Small Business Administration (SBA) loans

- do business start-up or machinery acquisition loans

- focus on first-time homebuyers

- focus on homebuyers in bankruptcy
  ... and the list goes on and on.

It is not advisable for you to try to do everything, even though that is what a lot of brokers do. Whenever someone asks them about a particular loan, whether it be for a personal residence or a commercial loan, they will say that they can do it, and then try to find out how.

The most successful brokers find a niche they feel comfortable with, and then dominate that niche. If someone in your town is regarded as the expert in financing homes over $1 million, then the people buying these homes, the builders building them, and the Realtors selling them will all come to this broker so that the deal goes through.

After you are done with your initial training, you should be focused on generating business for the rest of your career. There are many different ways to do this.

For example, working with only one Realtor who refers you one loan a month can put over $40,000 in your pocket per year. And you can work with as many Realtors as you want. But getting them to work with you is the hard part. Every loan officer in town goes after Realtors. If you set yourself apart from the others, you will have a better chance.

If you would like more information on exactly how to get Realtors to want to work with you, visit: **www.marketingtoagents.com.com**.

You also need to generate referrals from your past clients, friends, and family, but there are good ways to ask for business and bad ways to ask.

At our website, **www.mortgagebrokertraining.com**, one of our newest products is a marketing system that shows you

- why referrals are the easiest and cheapest way to get loans

- how to turn each client into a walking, talking billboard for your business

- how to handle each referral so it turns into multiple loans

Having a website is also a good way to generate customers. Direct mail and direct marketing can work wonders as well, if you do it right. But it is not as easy as it first appears.

Generating loans is the hardest part of the business. That's why we get paid the big bucks.

As you continue in this industry, make a serious effort to learn as much about marketing as you can. Anything you see that you consider good marketing can be adapted and used in the mortgage arena.

At the back of this book are descriptions of a few of the items we have available to help brokers generate as many loans as possible.

CHAPTER 11

Mortgage Banking

Mortgage banking is similar to mortgage brokerage, except that you are working for the lender.

In this chapter, we will go over some aspects of mortgage banking, in case you decide to go that route. Most positions at a mortgage bank are fixed-paycheck jobs. So if the thought of only working on commission scares you, but you still want to work in finance, this might be the way to go.

WHAT EXACTLY IS MORTGAGE BANKING?

The mortgage lending industry makes, sells, and services mortgages secured by residential, multi-family, and commercial real estate. The mortgage lending process is a complex series of interrelated activities, which offers you a number of different job opportunities. To help you better identify the best match for your interests and abilities, let's first review the various activities associated with mortgage lending.

- **Origination** is the creation of mortgage applications. Loan originators (loan officers and brokers) are the sales force in the real estate finance industry. Loan officers do the job of mortgage brokers for the lender. Whether a loan officer or a broker, the loan originator initiates the origination process by locating borrowers and making loan applications.

- **Processing** is the collection of documentation and verifications to support information provided on the loan application. Among the documents obtained by the processor are the appraisal, which confirms the value of the mortgaged property, and a credit report, which discloses the borrower's credit history.

- **Underwriting** is the evaluation of loan documentation to approve or deny the loan. During the evaluation process, the underwriter analyzes whether the loan represents an acceptable risk to the lender. An important aspect of the evaluation process is determining whether the loan meets the requirements that make it saleable to investors in the secondary mortgage market.

- **Closing** is the consummation of the loan transaction. The closing process involves the delivery of a deed, the signing of the note, and the disbursement of loan funds.

- **Warehousing** is the method by which most mortgage bankers fund the loans at closing. Warehousing involves short-term borrowing of funds from warehouse banks using permanent mortgage loans as collateral. The money borrowed from this line of credit is used to produce mortgage loans. Once the loans are sold to an investor on the secondary market, the mortgage banker replenishes the warehouse line, enabling it to use the funds to create more loans.

- **Shipping and delivery** is the packaging of closed loan files for delivery to an investor. This consummates the loan sale and all activities associated with loan production.

- **Secondary marketing** is the sale of closed loans to investors, the development and pricing of loan programs, and the management of the risk associated with funding mortgages. Normally, the sale to investors is arranged simultaneously with the origination of loans. Commitments are used to secure the future sale of loans and protect against interest rate changes that may occur between the dates of origination and sale.

- **Loan administration (servicing)** is the collection, recordation, and remittance of monthly mortgage payments to investors. Servicing also includes the maintenance of escrows to protect the property securing each loan.

CHAPTER 12

Commercial
Loans

Commercial lending involves the same real estate issues as residential lending, including borrower credit, underwriting, loan documentation, loan appraisal, loan sale, loan hedging, and loan administration. But the business aspects of commercial properties makes commercial lending more complicated, and it requires professionals with a slightly different skill set.

Commercial real estate is more than just the real estate; it also includes leasing of commercial real estate—houses, offices, warehouses, industrial sites, hotels, stores, apartment complexes, etc.

Even when buying and selling is involved, commercial real estate is ultimately focused on rent. Rent is the driving force of any commercial real estate project, because it provides the cash flow that supports the commercial real estate venture.

WHAT SKILLS DO I NEED?

Commercial mortgage lenders require more business education and analytical skills than do the residential lenders. Commercial lenders should also be well versed in spreadsheets, databases, graphical analysis, and geographic information systems.

HOW MUCH CAN I MAKE?

Commercial loan officers work on a 100% commission. Commercial loan officers with 1 to 3 years of experience earn between $48,000 and $64,750. With over 3 years of experience, commercial loan officers could make between $66,000 and $95,250 (**Source:** Department of Labor, *Occupational Outlook Handbook*).

CHAPTER 13

The Future of the Business

The future of the industry looks very bright indeed.

Home ownership is something that will never go out of style.

Everyone is telling people to own their own homes—the government, financial planners, investment gurus, and everybody in between.

Every few years, interest rates drop and there is a refinance boom. The year of 2003 was such a time. Everyone who owned a house wanted to refinance, and some people even did it twice as rates kept dropping.

While we don't see such booms every year, new housing continues to be strong and, with the government's support, homeowner initiatives will always be around.

In fact, the following HUD press release shows how the government will make it much easier for people to buy homes and thus increase our market.

BUSH ADMINISTRATION ANNOUNCES NEW HUD "ZERO DOWN PAYMENT" MORTGAGE

Initiative Aimed at Removing Major Barrier to Homeownership

Las Vegas—As part of President Bush's ongoing effort to help American families achieve the dream of homeownership, Federal Housing Commissioner John C. Weicher today announced that HUD is proposing to offer a "zero down payment" mortgage, the most significant initiative by the Federal Housing Administration in over a decade. This action would help remove the greatest barrier facing first-time homebuyers—the lack of funds for a down payment on a mortgage.

Speaking at the National Association of Home Builders' annual convention, Commissioner Weicher indicated that the proposal, part of HUD's Fiscal Year 2005 budget request, would eliminate the statutory requirement of a minimum three percent down payment for FHA-insured single-family mortgages for first-time homebuyers.

"Offering FHA mortgages with no down payment will unlock the door to homeownership for hundreds of thousands of American families, particularly minorities," said HUD's Acting Secretary Alphonso Jackson. "President Bush has pledged to create 5.5 million new minority homeowners this decade, and this historic initiative will help meet this goal."

Preliminary projections indicate that the new FHA mortgage product would generate about 150,000 homebuyers in the first year alone.

"This initiative would not only address a major hurdle to homeownership and allow many renters to afford their own home, it would help these families build wealth and become true stakeholders in their communities," said Commissioner Weicher. "In addition, it would help spur the production of new housing in this country."

For those who choose to participate in the Zero Down Payment program, HUD would charge a modestly higher insurance premium, which would be phased down over several years, and would also require families to undergo pre-purchase housing counseling.

HUD is the nation's housing agency committed to increasing homeownership, particularly among minorities; creating affordable housing opportunities for low-income Americans; and supporting the homeless, elderly, people with disabilities and people living with AIDS. The Department also promotes economic and community development as well as enforces the nation's fair housing laws. More information about HUD and its programs is available on the Internet at **http://www.hud.gov/** and **espanol.hud.gov**.

	Previous	Current
The homeownership rate in the third quarter 2003 (68.4%) was higher than the revised third quarter 2002 rate (68.0%). The homeownership rate in the West was higher than 1 year ago, while rates in the Northeast, Midwest, and South remained statistically unchanged.	68.0% 3rd. Qtr. 2002	68.4% 3rd. Qtr. 2003

Source: U.S. Census Bureau as of October 28, 2003.

CHAPTER 14

Training
Sources

SMALL BUSINESS ADMINISTRATION RESOURCES

Founded more than 45 years ago, the SBA has offices in 100 cities across the United States and the character to help small businesses start and grow. The SBA offers counseling and booklets on business topics, and administers a small-business loan guarantee program.

(To find your area's SBA office, check the white pages and telephone books in your region under "United States Government, Small Business Administration" or visit **www.sba.gov**)

The SBA offers numerous publications, services, and videos for starting and managing small businesses. Publications are available on products, ideas, inventions, financial management, management and planning, marketing, crime prevention, personal management, and other topics.

(The booklets can be purchased for 1 or 2 dollars each at SBA offices or from SBA publications, P.O. Box 30, Denver, c/o 80201. Ask first for SBA form 115 a, the small-business directory, that lists available publication and includes an order form. You can also get more info about the SBA and it's programs at **www.sba.gov**).

The Service Corps of Retired Executives (SCORE) is a national nonprofit association with the goal of helping small businesses. SCORE is sponsored by the SBA, and the local office is usually in or near that of the local SBA office. SCORE members—retired men and women, and those still active in their own business—donate their time and experience to countless individuals regarding small-business issues.

TAX INFORMATION RESOURCES

The U.S. Treasury Department, Internal Revenue Service (IRS) offers numerous small-business tax education program videos through its regional offices. Topics include depreciation, business use of your home, employment taxes, excise taxes, starting a business, partnership, self-employed retirement plans, Subchapter S corporations, and federal tax deposits.

If you're considering using a portion of your home as a business office, request Publication 587 from the IRS. It's free and will help you determine if your business qualifies for this option.

What business expenses are deductible? There's a long list. The best answers are found in the free publication offered by the IRS, business expenses Publication 535.

You can get all these resources play the contacting the IRS directly or visiting its web site at **www.irs.gov.**

WHAT IS CONTINUING EDUCATION?

Continuing education is a necessary part of the business, and with good reason. There are so many changes the industry goes through every year that, unless you constantly educate yourself, you will be left in the dust.

Most states with licenses also require that brokers spend a set amount of hours in classes every year. If you do not, you lose your license. Again, this is a good thing. If the continuing education requirement pertains to you, do not look at it as a chore. Instead, try to get the most out of it. There are so many things to know that no one can know everything. And the more you learn, the more professional you can be and the more people you can help.

MORTGAGE RESOURCES

The mortgage industry, though highly regulated, does not have that many sources for education and training, but this is changing. As more people come into the business, more schools and training programs are being established. Some are better than others.

My company, Kamrock Publishing, in partnership with MoneyTree Mortgage, is dedicated to helping mortgage professionals achieve all they desire. To do so, we have created our website **www.mortgagebrokertraining.com** with you in mind.

Our products include mortgage training manuals, credit repair manuals, marketing manuals, and other training products.

There are also a few magazines dedicated to the mortgage industry. If you are a member of your local association of mortgage brokers, you will receive its monthly magazine as well as NAMB's magazine, called *Broker*.

OTHER EDUCATION SOURCES:

www.originationnews.com
www.scotsmansguide.com
www.mortgagemag.com

In all these publications you will find advertisements for lenders, net branches, software vendors, credit report resellers, and any other vendors looking to sell to mortgage people.

$$$ CHAPTER 15 $$$
Other Questions

HOW DO I MOTIVATE MYSELF?

Motivation is key to success in this business. As a commissioned mortgage broker, you are your own boss. You control what you do with your time. It is very easy to spend an hour every day reading the newspaper instead of looking for new business.

There are certain things you need to do. Prospecting is one of these things. Without new loans, you will have no future income, and getting new loans is what you are paid to do.

If you have never been in total control of your time before, you might find that you do not have the discipline to work effectively.

But do not despair. It happens to all of us. There are many times where I spend too much time reading the news on the Internet instead of doing what I should be doing.

The way to overcome this is to have focus. Goofing off is OK, if you get done everything that needs to be done.

Ask yourself the following questions:

- Why am I working?

- What will I do with my extra money?

- What is it that I want more than anything else?

- How do I reach my goals?

- What are my goals?

These are hard questions. And if you have never asked yourself these questions before, you need to sit down and determine your answers. What you need to come up with is the thing that keeps you going. It will help motivate you when things get rough. I cannot lie to you and say that mortgage brokerage is an easy business. It is not. It is like everything else; if you put in the time needed you will succeed. But it will not be overnight, and it will not be easy.

So when times get tough, you need to keep focused on the big goals, your priorities, and your dreams. Without these, it is very easy to fall victim to the temptation to quit.

Many mortgage brokers do quit. They find that they cannot handle the freedom. They cannot handle not having someone telling them what to do all the time.

Being a mortgage broker is not a 9–5 job—at least not until you become successful. It is a 7-day-a-week job. If you have no loans and you get a hot lead, but the borrower can only meet you on Sunday, you will meet him on Sunday.

After you start doing well, you will not have to go running after borrowers. They will come after you. If you provide great service, the word will spread, and borrowers will go out of their way to work with you. But it won't happen in the beginning.

Sure, you do not have to wake up until noon, then can go home at 2:00 in the afternoon. And no one is going to say anything to you if you act that way. But when it comes time to pay the bills, you won't have any excuses.

ARE MORTGAGES A SEASONAL BUSINESS?

Mortgages are needed all the time. People move all the time. So mortgage brokerage is not a seasonal business in the traditional sense.

There are certain months that are better than others. The summer months are the busiest. Families with kids prefer to move in the summer so the kids do not have to miss school. December is a very slow month. With the holidays around the corner, very few people think about buying a new house in December.

Refinancing is another ball game completely. People refinance when rates go down. They want to take advantage of the new lower interest rates before they go back up. The year of 2003 was great for refinances. The whole year was very hot. Rates were at their lowest levels in years, and people took advantage of it.

Mortgage brokers were super busy refinancing everybody. Even people who had bought a house a year earlier were refinancing. Some people refinanced more than once in 2003. It was crazy. These times are called refinance booms. It is easy money for lenders and brokers. And like all good things, these times come to an end. By December 2003, unless they lived under a rock, everyone who was going to refinance had refinanced, so the boom dried up.

On the other hand, when rates are high, times are tough for mortgage brokers. In the 1980s, when rates were up to 16–17%, very few people bought houses, and no one refinanced. Hopefully, rates will not go up that much again for a long time.

Overall, the Federal Reserve has done a great job in the last two decades keeping interest rates low. The economy has been good, and real estate continues to appreciate.

Owning a home is still the American Dream. People will always want to buy houses, and the government makes it advantageous to buy a house instead of renting. All these factors show that mortgage brokers are not going anywhere. They will be around for a long time.

HOW DO I HIDE MY INEXPERIENCE?

Borrowers typically do not ask you how long you have been in the business. But if they find out that you are new, they may be turned off.

At first, you should solicit business from your family and friends. Since they know you, they will know that you just got into the business. But they shouldn't mind, especially when you assure them that a senior loan officer in your firm will oversee everything you are doing to make sure it goes smoothly.

The best way to seem experienced is to act experienced. Know the jargon. Know the paperwork. Know the loan programs that are most commonly used in your office. Study the business until you can "talk mortgage" fluently.

It will not take long. After just 2–3 loans you will know what to expect in most situations. After more loans it will become second nature to you.

If you have an office, decorate it with trophies and certificates. It doesn't matter what they are for. They are there just to show the borrowers that you are someone that has been recognized as being something special. They probably won't even take the time to see what the awards are for. But the awards being there will go along way in making them feel at ease with their loan in your hands.

Remember that a mortgage is the largest debt most people have, and their home is considered their most valuable asset.

WHY BUYING A HOME IS A GOOD IDEA

- **The Best Investment**

As a general rule, homes appreciate about 4–5% a year. Some years will be more, some less. The figure will vary from neighborhood to neighborhood, and region to region.

Five percent may not seem like that much at first. Stocks (at times) appreciate much more, and you could easily earn over the same return with a very safe investment in treasury bills or bonds.

But take a second look...

Presumably, if you bought a $200,000 house, you did not pay cash. You got a mortgage, too. Suppose you put as much as twenty percent down—that would be an investment of $40,000.

At an appreciation rate of 5% annually, a $200,000 home would increase in value $10,000 during the first year. That means you earned $10,000 with an investment of $40,000. Your annual "return on investment" would be a whopping twenty-five percent.

Of course, you are making mortgage payments and paying property taxes, along with a couple of other costs. However, since the interest on your mortgage and your property taxes are both tax deductible, the government is essentially subsidizing your home purchase.

Your rate of return when buying a home is higher than almost any other investment you could make.

- **Income Tax Savings**

  Because of income tax deductions, the government is subsidizing your purchase of a home. All of the interest and property taxes you pay in a given year can be deducted from your gross income to reduce your taxable income.

  For example, assume your initial loan balance is $150,000 with an interest rate of eight percent. During the first year you would pay $9,969.27 in interest. If your first payment is January 1, your taxable income would be almost $10,000 less—due to the IRS interest rate deduction.

  Property taxes are deductible, too. Whatever property taxes you pay in a given year may also be deducted from your gross income, lowering your tax obligation.

- **Stable Monthly Housing Costs**

  When you rent a place to live, you can certainly expect your rent to increase each year—or even more often. If you get a fixed-rate mortgage when you buy a home, you have the same monthly payment amount for 30 years. Even if you get an adjustable rate mortgage, your payment will stay within a certain range for the entire life of the mortgage—and interest rates aren't as volatile now as they were in the late 1970s and early 1980s.

Imagine how much rent might be 10, 15, or even 30 years from now? Which makes more sense?

FORCED SAVINGS

Some people are just lousy at saving money. A house is an automatic savings account. You accumulate savings in two ways. Every month, a portion of your payment goes toward the principal. Admittedly, in the early years of the mortgage, this is not much. Over time, however, it accelerates.

Second, your home appreciates. Average appreciation on a home is approximately 5%, though it will vary from year to year, and in some years may even depreciate. Over time, history has shown that owning a home is one of the very best financial investments.

- **Freedom & Individualism**

When you rent, you are normally limited in what you can do to improve your home. You have to get permission to make certain types of improvements. Nor does it make sense to spend thousand of dollars painting, putting in carpet, tile or window coverings when the main person who benefits is the landlord and not you.

Since your landlord wants to keep his expenses to a minimum, he or she will probably not be spending much to improve the place either.

When you own a home, however, you can do pretty much whatever you want. You get the benefits of any improvements you make, plus you get to live in an environment you have created, not some faceless landlord.

• **More Space**

Both indoors and outdoors, you will probably have more space if you own your own home. Even moving to a condominium from an apartment, you are likely to find you have much more room available—your own laundry and storage area, and bigger rooms. Apartment complexes are more interested in creating the maximum number of income-producing units than they are in creating space for each of the tenants.

If you are moving to a home for the first time, you are going to be very pleased with all the new space you have available. You may have to even buy more "stuff."

In the next chapter are some final words of advice to you.

CHAPTER 16

Do's and Don'ts

IF YOU HAVEN'T DECIDED TO BECOME
A BROKER YET:

DO think it over. Take a few days to weigh the pros and cons explained in this book. Talk to someone in the business and find out what he thinks about it.

DO NOT make a rush decision. Becoming successful will take some time. Making a career move is not something you decide to do over lunch.

DO read this book over again. Make sure you understand what will be required of you.

DO NOT make this decision without consulting your spouse or family. Sacrifices will have to be made by you and your family as well, so don't leave them out.

IF YOU HAVE DECIDED TO BECOME A MORTGAGE BROKER:

DO start right away. Don't waste time. Take action right away.

DO NOT worry if you made the right choice. Listen to your gut, your inner voice, your soul. It will never lead you astray.

DO read everything you can. Start reading about mortgage brokers right away.

DO NOT neglect your training.

DO visit mortgage lenders in your area. Pose as a potential borrower. Discover what they offer. See how they present the disclosures. Determine which approach you like best. Model yours after the one you choose.

DO NOT start working at the first company you come to. Research several companies before you decide.

DO read this book over. And this time, take notes.

DO make a list of everyone you know. Tell them of your decision, so you can ask them for business.

DO set clear goals. Make sure you know why you are choosing this profession.

DO have fun.

DO rely on me. Remember that my company and I are here to make your transition easy and to help you be as successful as possible.

We want to help you achieve everything you dream of. Visit our site, **www.mortgagebrokertraining.com**, regularly and subscribe to the free newsletter to keep up to date on happenings in the marketplace.

In order to provide a balanced view of the business, we asked a number of our mortgage broker customers to answer a few questions for us relating to the business. These are presented in the next chapter.

All the responses are from people active in the business. We tried to get as broad a mix as possible. We have interviews of company owners, branch managers, loan officers, and consultants. Some are very new (only a few months in the business), and some have been around for decades.

CHAPTER 17

Interviews

Every interview offers something. I have taken the liberty to highlight what I though were the most important points made in each interview, and in some I have added my own comments before the interview.

Please note: The opinions given in the interviews are those of the person interviewed. They are not necessarily the opinions of the author or the publisher. The answers given are meant to be guidelines and not specific advice. Please carefully weigh all options before following any advice given to you.

Also, an answer from one interviewee might contradict an answer from another. That is why we interviewed so many—to give you a complete feel of the business from insiders. Hopefully, by using this book you will be able to avoid the frustrations our panel endured.

Name: Jim Rainey
Title: Owner
Organization: RainWalk Financial Center
Place: Colorado Springs, CO
Email: rainwalkfin@aol.com

How long have you been in the mortgage brokerage business?
Three years.

What is your yearly loan volume?
$8–10 million.

What do you like best about your job?
Helping people achieve the American dream of home ownership.

What do you like least about your job?
Not being able to get a truly deserving couple financed in a timely manner.

What advice would you give a person starting today?
Make your focus helping people and not just making money. If you truly help people, the money will come.

Knowing what you know now, what would you have done differently in your mortgage career?
Learned much more about lead-generation resources early on.

Please describe your job.

Owner/Broker/Processor.

What one tool would you say is essential to a newcomer in the business?

Establishing realtor and banker referral sources.

Is there any other advice you would give?

Despite temptations to the contrary, maintain your integrity above reproach at all times and in all of your dealings with your clients, referral sources, lenders, and your colleagues.

Name: Drew Miranda
Title: Branch Manager
Organization: Icon Financial Group
Email: dmiranda@iconfinancial.com

How long have you been in the mortgage brokerage business?
Twelve years.

What is your yearly loan volume?
Greater than $20 million.

What do you like best about your job?
The ability to solve problems using creative funding sources and techniques.

What do you like least about your job?
Pushy realtors who truly don't understand what it takes to get some people approved.

What advice would you give a person starting today?
Once you're in the business there are plenty of people to help resolve problems and make the loan fund, but focus on marketing yourself from Day One; there is no one to teach you that and you can take that anywhere you go.

Knowing what you know now, what would you have done differently in your our mortgage career?
Invested more time in developing systems to automate the processes and generate more leads from my marketing efforts.

Please describe your job.
Responsible for the recruiting, and retainment of quality loan originators as well as providing them with the marketing systems they need to be successful.

What one tool would you say is essential to a newcomer in the business?
A solid marketing system must be in place, and you can't always depend on most companies to provide it.

Is there any other advice you would give?
Life is too short to work with people you don't enjoy working with, in an environment that you don't feel comfortable in, doing something you don't truly enjoy; and it will show in your performance.

Name: Robert Dawson, CRMS
Title: Vice President/Operations Manager
Organization: Buckeye Mortgage Group, Inc
Address: Akron, Ohio
Email: jacred22@aol.com

How long have you been in the mortgage brokerage business?
Nine years.

What is your yearly loan volume?
$25–30 million.

What do you like best about your job?
Helping first-time homebuyers realize the dream of home ownership. Especially the ones who don't think they can buy a home. The look in their eyes on closing day makes it all worthwhile.

What do you like least about your job?
The hours. I work an average of 65–70 hours per week. Also, not everyone whom I deal with moves as quickly as I like to. That gets frustrating.

What advice would you give a person starting today?
Find a good company and be a loan officer. That is where the money is, not in ownership. Develop Realtor sources and concentrate on purchase business. Treat people fairly and always tell the truth, even if it's bad news. Don't be greedy and always remember where you came from.

Knowing what you know now, what would you have done differently in your mortgage career?

Remained a loan officer instead of opening my own shop. Now I have the headaches of 30 loan officers, along with my own. Make 50–60% somewhere and close 30–40k per month. You do the math. It's a great living.

Please describe your job.

I run the day-to-day operations and am also the top producer in my company.

Is there any other advice you would give?

Work hard. Stay focused. And never get too high or too low.

This interview is of a wholesale account representative, not a mortgage broker. This man works for a lender to fund loans sent to him by mortgage brokers.

Name: Darrin L. Haug
Title: Northern California Top Account Executive
Organization: Planet Financial Services
Email: dar2exl@sbcglobal.net

How long have you been in the mortgage brokerage business?
Three years.

What is your yearly loan volume?
$3–5+ million per month.

What do you like best about your job?
The challenge, the pressure to perform, the freedom, and that I have a direct hand in helping people achieve their dreams of home ownership.

What do you like least about your job?
Come end month it gets a bit crazy as all brokers tend to wait until then. Probably more from fall-out at other lenders more than just procrastination.

What advice would you give a person starting today?
Know your guidelines and programs. Product knowledge is such a key. Be accountable, be available.

Knowing what you know now, what would you have done differently in your mortgage career?

Started sooner.

Please describe your job.

Wholesale Account Executive for a direct lender, purchasing residential loan packages

What one tool would you say is essential to a newcomer in the business?

Knowledge.

Is there any other advice you would give?

Just work smart, work long hours, and know your products and guidelines better than everyone else.

Name: Patsy Taylor
Title: Loan Originator
Organization: World Leadership Group
Email: pattaylor@wlgdirect.com

How long have you been in the mortgage brokerage business?
Six months.

What do you like best about your job?
Helping clients who are in the refinance market harness the power of their mortgage. I am excited about new home purchasers because we educate these clients about what type of home loan programs to shop for.

What do you like least about your job?
It is very time consuming.

What advice would you give a person starting today?
Get excited. Stay focused and put God first, family second, and you will never be last!!

Knowing what you know now, what would you have done differently in your mortgage career?
I would have started a lot sooner than I did.

Please describe your job.
My job title is that of Loan Originator. It is my responsibility to create my own clientele. I help a potential client find the best

loan program to fit his or her needs. When that loan is found I then forward it to the loan processor. This can be done electronically via the internet.

What one tool would you say is essential to a newcomer in the business?
A desk or laptop computer!!

Is there any other advice you would give?
Yes. I would hope that people understand the importance of getting a big 30-year mortgage and never pay it off. Take advantage of the interest-only and cash-flow programs. Get into a property with less money down, and invest the difference.

Name: Robert McAvoy
Title: Branch Manager
Organization: MortgageAll Express
Address: Hampstead, NH
Email: rwmcavoy@juno.com

How long have you been in the mortgage brokerage business?
Six years.

What do you like best about your job?
I always get a nice feeling in helping buyers obtain financing for their first home. Also, being able to help people refinance so they can either start a business, do home improvements, help their children pay for college, and other emergencies makes you feel your job is important.

What do you like least about your job?
Not being able to help people because they have such damaged credit and they are not willing to take your advice on how they can improve it enough to be able to help them. Most of these people have such a bad attitude and feel the world owes them a living.

What advice would you give a person starting today?
READ, READ, and READ some more. Read everything you can get your hands on about the mortgage industry. Learn as

many mortgage programs and options as you can. People want to do business with someone who they feel knows what he is doing.

Knowing what you know now, what would you have done differently in your mortgage career?
I would have started sooner. I spent many years as a real estate agent. I enjoyed real estate but you have much better control of your time in the mortgage industry.

Please describe your job.
I am a branch manager and enjoy seeing the happy faces of our satisfied customers.

What one tool would you say is essential to a newcomer in the business?
PC skills.

Is there any other advice you would give?
Stay in touch with the people you have helped. Keep your name in front of them monthly, and you will see your referrals increase dramatically.

Name: Mr. Shamun "Shamoon" Mahmud
Title: Mortgage Consultant
Organization: Allied Home Mortgage
Email: shamun.mahmud@520LOAN.com

How long have you been in the mortgage brokerage business?
One year.

What do you like best about your job?
In a phrase, I love helping consumers live the American Dream. To see the joy in a person's eyes, when they take delivery of their home . . .Well, I still get a warm feeling.

What do you like least about your job?
Going back to the customer to ask for more information because "so-and-so" lender requires it for their new programs.

What advice would you give a person starting today?
Begin personal marketing as soon as you get started in the field. Start networking with EVERYONE you know, whether they are business or personal contacts. Offer good advice asking nothing in return. Offer to consult people on their current loan offers from other companies. If they are good offers, tell them so and congratulate them on their savvy!

Knowing what you know now, what would you have done differently in your mortgage career?

Never compromise your ideals. Under-promise and over-deliver. I should have started sooner.

Please describe your job.

Mortgage Consultant. I am more of a rainmaker than an Loan Officer.

What one tool would you say is essential to a newcomer in the business?

Act! database software.

Is there any other advice you would give?

Network with realtors. Start with introductory mail. Follow up with voicemail broadcasts and faxes.

Name: Michael W. Schneiderman
Title: Senior Mortgage Consultant
Organization: Advanced Mortgage Solutions
Address: Highland Park, NJ
Email: mschnei244@aol.com

How long have you been in the mortgage brokerage business?
Twenty years.

What do you like best about your job?
Being able to better explain the various programs to the client.

What do you like least about your job?
Sometimes, no matter how many times you explain the various products, the client decides to take another one at a higher rate.

What advice would you give a person starting today?
Make sure that you fully understand the mortgage application (1003) and supported documents.

Knowing what you know now, what would you have done differently in your mortgage career?
Had a web site sooner that would allow the individuals (potential customers) to see what is available.

Please describe your job.
Senior mortgage consultant.

What one tool would you say is essential to a newcomer in the business?

A mortgage calculator. Especially the HP 19B II, which I have been using for over 20 years along with the printer.

Is there any other advice you would give?

Attend the various seminars in the field and keep talking to other mortgage bankers or brokers about the subject matter.

Name: Vida Bridges
Title: Loan Officer
Organization: Vida Bridges Brokerage Services
Email: vidabridges@aol.com

How long have you been in the mortgage brokerage business?
Two years.

What is your yearly loan volume?
$1 million.

What do you like best about your job?
Flexibility, the chance to help my clients repair their credit and get their financial life under control. Learning new things about the financial services industry.

What do you like least about your job?
The lack of training from brokers, once you are signed up with them. Also, how brokers give loan officers low commissions with little assistance. I have been very frustrated throughout my career so far, but now I know the process and have begun to self-study.

What advice would you give a person starting today?
To learn the 1003 and how it controls the whole transaction. Get a copy of the stacking order for a file. Develop a good team consisting of title companies, real estate agents, appraisers,

lenders, and veteran loan officers whom you can ask occasional questions.

Knowing what you know now, what would you have done differently in your mortgage career?
I would have studied marketing to get a good stream of clients. Do more research about companies (where you are thinking of working) and shadow them before signing up to see if there is a fit.

Please describe your job.
Marketing to get customers, doing quick applications to see if the client will qualify, completing the 1003 loan application, running credit reports, getting loan approvals, doing title search, getting income document, bank statements, doing verifications, ordering appraisals, getting stipulation, and closing loans.

What one tool would you say is essential to a newcomer in the business?
Networking.

Is there any other advice you would give?
I think this is a great thing to be doing. When I first started, I thought of it as a game. I could see the frustration on all of our faces. If it is a game, it can be fun from the beginning, instead of full of stress.

Name: Nicole Donn
Title: Branch Manager
Organization: US Financial Mortgage
Email: RELoan2000@aol.com

How long have you been in the mortgage brokerage business?
Twenty-one years.

What is your yearly loan volume?
$24–$40 million.

What do you like best about your job?
I like being able to use my creativity to help people become homeowners and/or rearrange their finances so they are able to live more fully.

What do you like least about your job?
I have been known to work way too many hours and I am not crazy about managing people.

What advice would you give a person starting today?
To learn as much as possible about the loan products. It should be easy to understand and if it is not, perhaps this is not the right field for you. Also, every minute not working on a loan should be used to either learn about loans, self-improvement or, most importantly, business development.

Knowing what you know now, what would you have done differently in your mortgage career?

I would have screened new loan officer recruits more carefully. I have wasted a lot of time training people who were not well suited for the job.

Please describe your job.

I am the branch manager/owner/primary originator of a net branch.

What one tool would you say is essential to a newcomer in the business?

Work hard networking with Realtors and other business professionals until you have a reliable, consistent lead source. Stay in touch with existing customers.

Is there any other advice you would give?

Although the mortgage business is not for everyone, for those of us who have the aptitude, it is a great way to make a living. Do not bait and switch. Under-promise and over-deliver. This makes you look good and makes the transaction much less stressful. Be honest and don't gouge. Repeat and referral business is the easiest business to get and, with the built in trust factor, the easiest business to close.

Name: Jeff Shaffer
Title: Loan Officer
Organization: Green Leaf Mortgage
Address: Montgomery Village, MD
Email: jeffshaffer00@yahoo.com

How long have you been in the mortgage brokerage business?
Two years.

What is your yearly loan volume?
$12 million.

What do you like best about your job?
Helping my clients.

What do you like least about your job?
Dealing with over-demanding real estate agents.

What advice would you give a person starting today?
Be very organized.

Knowing what you know now, what would you have done differently in your mortgage career?
Started years ago!!

Please describe your job.
Loan Officer—main function is to sell and close loans.

What one tool would you say is essential to a newcomer in the business?

A strong loan processor.

Is there any other advice you would give?

Only deal with lenders that are customer service-oriented. We as loan officers have hundreds of choices of lenders. You must be very picky in choosing your lenders.

Name: Richelle McKim
Title: Mortgage Broker
Organization: Real Estate Mortgage Warehouse
Email: morningstarfin@juno.com

How long have you been in the mortgage brokerage business?
Eight months.

What is your yearly loan volume?
$1.5 million.

What do you like best about your job?
It's part-time. I can work it around my child.

What do you like least about your job?
On closing days, I might be on the phone 4 hours trying to baby-sit the details. It's hard to find a babysitter for a last-minute application or closing.

What advice would you give a person starting today?
Advertise once-a-month to every address you have. Use a title company's advertising department. Don't use cheesy materials. Give something to your customers that is valuable to them, not just a recipe in the mail.

Knowing what you know now, what would you have done differently in your mortgage career?
Advertised more often.

Please describe your job.
Loan officer.

What one tool would you say is essential to a newcomer in the business?
Learning the lingo, 10-o-3 (1003), etc. Hooking up with a good Realtor, and being flexible.

Is there any other advice you would give?
Every closing ends up being a rush, and no closing goes smoothly. Price your loans so that if your client goes to somebody else, the other mortgage broker will hardly make a dime, but price them so that you have some room to take out of your back-end for errors (pricing adjustments, lock extensions, etc.).

Name: Dana D. Cubert
Title: Account Executive/Loan Originator
Organization: Heartland Home Finance
Address: Indianapolis, IN
Email: dcubert@heartlandfinance.com

How long have you been in the mortgage brokerage business?
Four and a half years.

What is your yearly loan volume?
Between $4 and 5 million.

What do you like best about your job?
Helping customers save money on their mortgage refinancing.
Getting to know my customers.

What do you like least about your job?
Not being able to help a customer who drastically needs financial relief on a monthly basis.

What advice would you give a person starting today?
Do not get frustrated. It is a killer to our line of business. Make sure you have a full pipeline (potential loans), because something will always come up when a loan officer is closing loans. Originate and originate. That is where you keep the stress to a minimum. Stress is unavoidable in our business.

Knowing what you know now, what would you have done differently in your mortgage career?

1. Taken advantage of learning more products available with different lenders, and that would have been more money earned with each loan I touched.

2. Attached second mortgages and lines of credit with each first mortgage refinancing.

3. Debt relief is a seller for most first mortgage customers.

Please describe your job.

Loan originator, loan officer, account executive. And I have processed most of my own loans.

What one tool would you say is essential to a newcomer in the business?

Telephone, calculator, and scratch paper. Learn the business by scratch and don't rely on a computer to get around in a loan.

Is there any other advice you would give?

Originate, go out and see your customers, and learn all products available to you. This is your money and every customer is going to be doing a loan with someone. It might as well be you. Be confident, and it will come out in you.

Name: Stacia Hamilton
Title: Mortgage Advisor
Organization: Equilliance Mortgage
Address: Orlando, Florida
Email: Stacia.Hamilton@equilliance.com

How long have you been in the mortgage brokerage business?
One year.

What do you like best about your job?
Previously I was a financial advisor. I use this background to get a whole overview of what a person needs, not just throw them into a mortgage. I enjoy helping people find the right mortgage to fit them and their new home.

What do you like least about your job?
I dislike the bad reputation many mortgage brokers have brought the business. There are a LOT of bad brokers out there throwing people into loans that will cause a foreclosure blowout in a year or two. I've watched too many brokers do it for the money and not for the client.

What advice would you give a person starting today?
I obtained my license in April of 2004, so as a newbie myself, I would advise people to find a well-established broker house. Here they would learn the in's and out's of basic mortgaging.

They should also look for support and training because you learn nothing about mortgaging in the 3-day mortgage school. I would tell them to take a year or two to absorb as much as they could from the broker house and then look to move on. I wish someone had told me this in the beginning. I started with a small mortgage company and I have tried to teach myself how to mortgage and have read as many books as I can on the subject, but without formal training it has taken me longer to get the "hang of the business" than it might have otherwise. It's a lot more frustrating learning from mortgage to mortgage then to have a trainer or even a mentor. However, I would also warn them not to stay in a broker house too long as there are more exciting and interesting aspects to this job than what a broker house will teach you.

Knowing what you know now, what would you have done differently in your mortgage career?

1. Started with a large company taking a smaller commission (50% of something is more than 70% of nothing).

2. Found a mentor.

3. Started W2 (as a paid employee) and moved into 1099 (independent contractor).

4. Looked for support and training over commission.

5. Set up a marketing campaign early on.

Please describe your job.

I write prescription mortgages to help ease home buying pain. We look at the whole financial picture along with the present and future plans and goals to prescribe the perfect mortgage for our clients.

What one tool would you say is essential to a newcomer in the business?

A mentor or trainer. The learning curve is so big in the beginning for this business it can be very overwhelming and intimidating. Having someone to turn to, to ask questions of, and get advice from is essential to not only becoming a mortgage broker but also surviving the first couple of years.

Is there any other advice you would give?

Just do it and hang in there. It's tough to get started but easy once you get it. Also, network, network, network. I attend at least 4 networking events a week to get my name and face out there to the public. Go to leads groups, happy hours, luncheons, special events, fundraisers, social groups, and specific member meetings, such as women's groups, minority groups, religious groups, etc. Just get out there and meet people, make referral partners, and get leads. The leads can turn into loans, which can turn right back into referrals!!

Name: Steve Soccio
Title: Branch Manager
Organization: Louviers Mortgage Corporation
Address: Newark, DE

How long have you been in the mortgage brokerage business?
One year.

What is your yearly loan volume?
$3 million.

What do you like best about your job?
Knowing that I am providing a resource to help people fulfill a dream of saving money or owning a home.

What do you like least about your job?
Having to decline potential clients.

What advice would you give a person starting today?
Be prepared to do what it takes to become successful.

Knowing what you know now, what would you have done differently in your mortgage career?
I would have spent more time on education and product development.

Please describe your job.

Being able to offer a convenient way to comparison shop for a loan in a secure, pressure-free environment. Consumers don't have to leave home or spend hours on the phone to get the best rates, because I will do all the legwork for them.

What one tool would you say is essential to a newcomer in the business?

Dedication is the one tool that covers the amount of time you spend developing yourself, client base, education, and your overall success

Is there any other advice you would give?

Research the business completely. Every aspect of it.

Name: Donn S. Luthanen
Title: Branch Manager
Organization: Nationwide Equities Corp
Email: dluthanen@nwecorp.com

How long have you been in the mortgage brokerage business?
Two and a half years.

What do you like best about your job?
The ability to be creative through methods of problem solving to tailor loans to a PARTICULAR person's needs. Each person is different, and methods need to be learned everyday to do the job correctly.

What do you like least about your job?
Knowing that there are plenty of people in the industry who have immoral practices. This creates great apprehension for clients to come over in the beginning of the mortgage process. The industry needs to pride itself on becoming recognized as a profession like doctors or lawyers.

What advice would you give a person starting today?
Be honest, learn your products, find computer software that speeds your process, and do not be greedy on one file to look for referrals. Learn to use veracity in all aspects of your business.

Knowing what you know now, what would you have done differently in your mortgage career?

1. I would have worked with a large company first to learn how and what I needed to create my business and goals.

2. I would have spent more time in the beginning on bringing new business to the table than structuring the office for "what might be."

Please describe your job.

Manager: I over see all operations of the business. I pride myself on being compliant with the law and make sure the employees see the importance of it. I also educate them myself.

What one tool would you say is essential to a newcomer in the business?

A software program to database clients, a system to build referral sources from past clients (mailings or emails—thank you cards), a cell phone to be available whenever you can be. Only use a few lenders so you do not waste time looking for the best deal through hundreds of places. Time is the most valuable asset you have.

Is there any other advice you would give?

Read the laws from the banking department. Go to websites for mortgage professionals and spend the time to read what other people are doing. Read product guidelines. BIGGEST TIP: DO NOT RELY ON OTHER PEOPLE FOR INFORMA-TION. Look it up yourself.

INDEX

A
achievement, 95
activities, 19
adaptability, 94
administration, loan, 106
advertising, 89
Alabama requirements, 67
Alaska requirements, 67
applications, loan, 79
appraisers, 83–84
Arizona requirements, 67
Arkansas requirements, 67
attitude, importance of, 91–93
attorneys, real estate, 85

B
banks, 44
benefits of home ownership, 127–128
books
  How To Jump Start Your Mortgage Career, 26
  How To Make Your Credit Sparkle, 84
  Residential Loan Origination Made Easy, 84
Bridges, Vida, interviewee, 150–151
business generation, 97–102
busy times, 121–123

C
California requirements, 67
challenges, 9–10

classes. *see* education
clients, acquiring, 99–102
closing, 80, 105
collection officers
  earnings, 38–40
  education, 35–36
  employment, 34
  job description, 33
  job outlook, 36–38
  working conditions, 33–34
Colorado requirements, 67
commercial banks, 44
commercial real estate, 107–108
commissions, 20, 23, 55–56, 60
competition, 88–90
conforming loans, 20, 42
Connecticut requirements, 67
contact information. *see* websites
conventional loans, 42
costs, 19, 21–23, 54, 73
credit reports, 84
credit scoring, 31–32, 37, 84
credit unions, 44–45
Cubert, Dana D., interviewee, 158–159
Cuomo, Andrew, 47–48

D
Dawson, Robert, interviewee, 138–139
decision to become mortgage broker, 129–130
Delaware requirements, 67

Marketing Materials You Need to Succeed

**ATTENTION MORTGAGE BROKERS:
NOT BEING PROPERLY TRAINED CAN COST YOU
THOUSANDS IN LOST COMMISSIONS!**

As a mortgage originator, you make a living by writing up applications.

But you can never reach your true potential if you don't do it right.

Residential Mortgage Loan Origination Made Easy has been written to teach you how to originate loans and get them closed, so you can get paid more often.

Knowledge results in more confidence and more money. The better trained you are, the higher your tax bracket can be. Plus, borrowers flock to the individuals who are confident and who can answer their questions right away. Your referral business will skyrocket as your knowledge increases.

Put yourself in the borrower's shoes. Who would you do business with: a cool, confident professional, or a nervous rookie who cannot answer even basic questions?

YOU CANNOT AFFORD TO BE A ROOKIE

Not in this game. Because losing in this game means losing your house, your car, and your job.

You have chosen to be a mortgage professional and that's what you need to be. The better trained you are, the more professional you can be.

This Manual Gives You The Basic Mortgage Training You Need To Be Professional.

Over 180 pages of confidence-building, image-enhancing material is within your grasp. Over 17 chapters that cover all you need to know to be the best mortgage originator around. Once you complete this manual, your co-workers who have been in business for years will be amazed that you are more knowledgeable than they are!

This book is a must for all loan officers originating loans. It is both an excellent training manual and a wonderful reference book of mortgage laws, terms, and techniques. Not only is it filled with useful information, but you also get easy to use forms, agreements, and worksheets.

> *When I first got my license, I was nervous before every conversation. I was afraid someone would ask me something that I didn't know. After reading your book, I now know what to say. I can now answers questions that used to trip me up and cost me loans. I found in your book what I did not find anywhere else. Thank you so much.*

—Alan Sans, Detroit, Michigan

So how can you be a successful mortgage originator?

TO BE A SUCCESSFUL MORTGAGE ORIGINATOR THERE ARE 3 THINGS YOU MUST KNOW

Item 1: Know the laws and guidelines involved in mortgage originating.

Item 2: Know how to take an application, and qualify and place a loan.

Item 3: Get the loan closed.

This book teaches you all three.

Item 1: Chapters 5–8 cover all the laws concerning your mortgage originations, as well as all FNMA loan guidelines.

Item 2: Chapters 9–13 teach you exactly what to do and what to say to customers from an initial meeting through pre-qualification and through application. <u>This includes a line-by-line explanation of both the Good Faith Estimate and the 1003 Loan Application.</u>

Item 3: Chapters 14–17 help you understand what else is involved to close the loan—from locking the loan, to ordering the appraisal, to sending out verifications, to how long it should all take. Everything is covered.

But how can you be sure that you will know what to do when the time comes?

Good Question.

That's what Section 4 is for. It contains two exercises taken from real life situations for you to complete.

Even after 3 years in the business, I was still running into road blocks that kept my loans from closing. I had plenty of leads, but most of them did not qualify. That is, until I got your manual. You showed me exactly how to place my loans to get more of them approved. In the first 3 months after getting the manual, I closed 6 loans that I otherwise would have lost. That's $9,000 I would have been without!

—Ryan Thomas, High Point, North Carolina

So what's left to know? Nothing.

This book will show you how to:

- Get your loans approved by FNMA.

- Do a full-fledged pre-qualification in less than 5 minutes.

- Fill out a Good Faith Application with your eyes closed.

- Complete an entire 1003 application and understand it thoroughly—this includes exercises.

- Complete all FNMA requirements for the property and the borrower.

- Use the tools you need to succeed in this business. You already have most of them; the rest you can get from this manual.

- Know the differences between the various mortgage loans available today.

- Understand and interpret rate sheets.

- Obey all laws involved to keep you out of jail.

- Understand B, C, and D markets.

- Read a review of the most widely used mortgage products available today.

- Know the most frequently asked questions by borrowers and their answers.

  Wow, I can't believe the stuff I didn't know about until I read a friend's copy of your training manual. I have to get one for myself.

  —Alonzo Santiago, Boulder, Colorado

You will learn:

- Why being a mortgage originator is one of the last professions remaining that you can enter with little out of your pocket and unlimited income potential.

- What you will need to get started.

- Who should you work for—lender or broker—strengths and weaknesses of both are discussed.

- How and what wrong questions asked to a borrower can land you in serious trouble with the law.

- How the lending system works from the inside out—a thorough explanation of primary and secondary markets.

- Which laws affect mortgage origination and how to abide by them.

- How to lock a rate and explain its importance to borrowers.

- How to read and interpret a credit report.

- How appraisals are completed and the methods used.

- How long a mortgage should take to close and how long each step takes.
- Why people use mortgage brokers—and it's not the rate!
- The ins and outs of RESPA, Reg-Z, and ECOA.

Who is this book for?

The New Kid On The Block—for a jump-start in the business.

The Old Pro—for an invaluable reference.

The Training Manager—for a training supplement.

The Processor—for an inside look at what loan officers know.

The Real Estate Agent—for a tool to improve communication with loan officers and make sure everything is being done properly so the deals close.

Anyone Looking To Get Into The Business—for a behind-the-scenes look at what it's like and what to expect, as well as detailed instructions on what to do once you are in the business.

> *Your book is on the top shelf of my bookcase. I know exactly where it is whenever I need to look up something. Even after doing a few hundred loans, there is no way I am going to remember all the legal mumbo-jumbo. And I don't want to. So whenever I need to look up something, I just pick up your book. Make sure to contact me when it is updated.*

—Lourdes Sanchez, Miami, Florida

The Bottom Line . . .Whether you are already in the mortgage business, or looking to get in, the information in this book will make you a Mortgage Origination Expert.

If you want to be a real professional mortgage loan originator, this book is for you.

Just check out the table of contents and see for yourself all
that's included.

SECTION 1: SO YOU WANT TO BE A MORTGAGE LOAN ORIGINATOR?

SECTION 2: AN INTRODUCTION TO MORTGAGE LENDING

SECTION 3: IN THE FIELD

SECTION 4: LET'S SEE WHAT YOU GOT
Exercise 1

Exercise 2

Appendix 1:   Disclosures

Appendix 2:   Verification and Other Forms

Glossary

Before we send you to the order form, we wanted to let you know that along with the manual we are providing several
FREE BONUSES!
Bonus #1: Mortgage Broker Marketing On a Shoestring Budget—How To Jump Start Your Income As A Mortgage Broker For Less Than $200.

This FREE report details the most powerful methods of marketing known to the mortgage industry. We use all these techniques in our office every day, and they work. If you are looking for a way to have more leads than you can handle, use just a couple of the methods discussed in this report. It is jam-packed with ideas that for under $200 can be implemented today.

We have seen marketing "gurus" charge hundreds of dollars for this same information. We ourselves charge $39.95 for this report by itself. You get it for FREE along with the manual. We want you to be super successful, and we feel that the manual and the report put you head and shoulders above 95% of your competition.

Implementing just one of these methods will bring in enough in commissions to pay for the manual a thousand times.

We left nothing back. We put in everything you need to know. Even if you buy the manual just for this report, it is worth every penny and them some. You'll see.

Bonus #2: Secrets of the Richest People—Find out how the rich think—why they are more successful than other people, when they all have challenges and problems just like everybody else. This FREE report will open your eyes. It helps you identify what you haven't done yet to be rich. It teaches you what you can do to BE rich. This is our motivational Bonus. It puts you in the right frame of mind to go out and implement the strategies we teach on the manual and Bonus #1.

Following our strategies, you will be armed with the information you need to make a lot of money in this business. But if your mind is not ready to handle it, you can sabotage your own efforts. There is a proper way to "think rich." This report shows you how. Sold by itself for $39.95, it is yours free.

Bonus #3: How to Influence People and Win Them Over—This FREE report details exactly what you need to do to attract more clients. The more people like you, the better your chances they will do business with you. So you need to know how to get through their "barriers" and into their good graces. If you don't have a bubbly personality and aren't the star of every party you go to, you need this report.

One of the most important things in mortgage marketing is being remembered. This report will show you how to be remembered by everyone you meet. Sold by itself for $39.95, it is yours free.

Residential Mortgage Loan Origination Made Easy is distributed by Kamrock Publishing LLC, in consultation with MoneyTree Mortgage in Houston.

It was originally developed as a training manual for our brokers only. A couple years ago, one of our new brokers took the manual to a yearly convention of the Texas Association of Mortgage Brokers. At the convention, the manual was accidentally lost. It turned out that a head trainer from a larger company had picked it up and thumbed through it. After getting rave reviews from this person, we decided to share it with mortgage brokers nationwide.

No one in my office could believe that I was able to make $9,000 on my first loan! But I did. And it's all thanks to what I got out of your book. Keep up the great work.
—Timothy Moore, Irvine, California

At first I thought you were asking too much for your manual. So I ordered one from someone else. Some of the information in that book was totally wrong and out of date. But I didn't know better so I did what that book said. Because of it, I got fired from the company I was at, and almost got sued by the borrower. I learned the hard way that it's better to pay a few extra dollars and get the best.
—Author asked for name not to be revealed.

Up until now we haven't told you how much it is.

Take a look at what is being offered and make a guess as to how much this book is worth to you. It can take years off your learning curve if you are new in the business.

The average loan you make should net you about $2,000. You will definitely get one more loan from the material in the manual and the FREE REPORTS.

If you sat through a seminar that covered all this material, it would take at least 3 days. That is how long it takes us to cover all this material when training new brokers. How much is your time worth?

How about the loans you could lose if you don't get this information? One broker earned $9,000 within a few months because of what he learned from this manual.

We could easily charge a few hundred dollars and it would still be a bargain.

But in order the make it affordable to all brokers and loan officers, we priced it so low that there is no excuse for not having this valuable resource in your library ready to answer all your questions.

You get the complete 180+ page manual, the jam-packed Free Reports, and our unconditional 30-day money-back guarantee.

THE GUARANTEE

We want you to be a Mortgage Origination Pro. We're happy only if you are really happy, so here's our guarantee to you. If you feel that Residential Mortgage Loan Origination Made Easy does not deliver everything we say it does, simply tell us you want your money back within 30 days.

We'll refund your money immediately, and you get to keep the FREE Reports!

- No reason required

- No exceptions
- No strings attached

I've worked in the mortgage industry for ten years. I first saw your manual about three years ago, and knew right away it was simply the best manual of its kind in the marketplace. Today, when I hire a new broker, the first thing I do is make them read through your entire manual. Doing this has saved me countless hours of training them. Keep up the good work.

—Mike Tong, Baltimore, MD

Where were you guys when I first started? It took me 3 years to learn everything my son learned by reading your manual in two days!

—Russell White, Dayton, OH

I just got my license two weeks before getting your manual, and I didn't have a clue of what to do first. Thank God your sales letter got to me. Because of your manual, I stopped myself from making a couple of huge mistakes: 1. Working for the wrong company and 2. How to market without spending lots of money. Thank you so much!

—Yammy Rodriguez, Miami, Florida

I have worked at 5 different mortgage companies in the past 8 years. And I know of no one who knows more about mortgage origination than Abby Kamadia. I thought I knew a lot when I came to work for him. But he blew me away. And he has put everything you need to know into this manual. There is nothing that you can do that will help your career better than to read this thing cover to cover. Just do it.

—A. Aribani, Houston, Texas

I wish all brokers sending me loans had this manual. I spend most of my day fixing items in files that have been submitted wrongly and answering basic questions by untrained brokers. Please Abby, just give it away to everyone!

—Eddy Osborn, Wholesale Lending Division, National Lender

Remember Our Promise:
You will close more loans or your money back
Yours in success,
Abby Kamadia
MoneyTree Mortgage
P.S. A six-figure income starts with one simple step—being committed to yourself and ordering this manual. ORDER TODAY!

To Order:
By Phone: Call us at 713-782-5626.
Have your credit card ready.
Online: www.mortgagebrokertraining.com
By Mail: Mail your check or money order to:
Kamrock Publishing
7447 Harwin St, Suite 218
Houston, TX 77036

WARNING: 82% OF LOAN OFFICERS DO NOT PRODUCE ENOUGH LOANS TO LAST MORE THAN 2 YEARS IN THE MORTGAGE BUSINESS.

. . . what 1 simple step can you take to make sure this doesn't happen to you?

The Jump Start Your Mortgage Career E-Class is your next step to mortgage success.

Here is a taste of some of the things you will learn in the online course:

- A way to double your closings without any extra leads.

- How to set up your business so that if you took a one-month vacation you would still have a thriving business when you got back.

- Seven ways to get Realtors to give you ALL their business.

- The 7 Steps I use when someone tells me to lower my fees.

- How to get all the FREE advertising you want.

- How "the halo effect" can get you loads of qualified prospects seeking you out.

- The one technique that brings in more referrals than all others combined.

- How to generate customers with zero acquisition cost.

- How NOT to get business from Realtors. (Why most loan officers waste their time and money and never get any business from Realtors.)

- Sixty-nine ways to market to borrowers that work.

- Don't just master your business career, but learn to master the 5 other areas of your life for true peace of mind.

- Over 3 dozen marketing ideas that cost less than $100 each to implement and work like gangbusters!

- When to flaunt your personality in your business and when not to—Do this properly and customers will flock to you. Do it wrong, and you will offend them.
- How "souvenirs" can make you hundreds of thousands in commissions.
- Why, according to *Sales And Marketing* magazine, 80% of all people who inquire about a product buy within 1 year—but not from the company that made the original contact, and how to make sure this never happens to you.
- Why you should never market to "anyone who wants a mortgage".
- The #1 most important business secret in the mortgage biz. Ignore this and you are condemning yourself to a life of gut-wrenching prospecting forever.
- And many more.

Twenty-two lessons taught by your own personal instructor. It doesn't matter if today is your first day in the mortgage business or if this is your thirty-fifth year. If you could use more business this course is for you.

Top Producers all have one thing in common: they know how to market themselves. That is what this course will teach you.

We guarantee that this course will work for you or your money back. And we have made it affordable for all loan officers. In fact, you should get at least 3–4 loans from what you learned in the course even before you finish the course!

Give yourself a head start. Learn from the mistakes and successes of others. Jump Start Your Mortgage Career Today.

Learn more about the class and how to enroll at
www.JumpStartYourMortgageCareer.com

"THE AMAZING SECRETS OF BUILDING A MULTI-MILLION DOLLAR MORTGAGE BUSINESS FROM SCRATCH."

You are sitting at your desk, daydreaming about your upcoming trip to Vegas this weekend, when an associate comes over to talk to you. "Boy, I just hate rate shoppers! Arrrrrr! Just lost another loan because somebody quoted a quarter percent less then I did. I was counting on that loan to pay my rent this month," he blurts. Before you can answer, your phone rings. The voice on the line says, "Hi, my name is Jim Smith. I am about to put an offer in to buy a house. I work with Loren Alder; she said would kill me if I didn't get my loan from you. How soon should we meet to get started?"

Imagine if there was a group of people, say 300 of them. And these 300 people lived normal lives. They did everything the way everybody else does them: work at a normal job, live in an average house, have kids who go to school. Just normal people.

Except that whenever these people need a mortgage they have to get it from you.

They have no choice in the matter. As soon as they think of the word mortgage, their brains cause a chemical reaction so that the only person they can think about is you. Would that help your business? I should say so. If we look at the averages, 10% of these people are going to move every year. That's 30 loans a year coming to you, guaranteed. This is the power of *Referrals on Demand*.

Here are even more benefits of the system:

- **Have a steady stream of loans each and every month from your personal sales force.**

- Instead of being dependent upon advertising for business, you will have Realtors, financial planners, and other business owners dependent upon you for referrals.
- You will be in control of your business and life by having so many leads and loans, you only have to work with the people who want to work with you.
- You do not need to spend money on consumer marketing because you will be able to have leads come to you FREE of charge.
- There is nothing for you to write, create, or spend time or money developing. Everything you need is included.
- You eliminate the need to compete with other lenders because borrowers will be sent to you already pre-sold on the idea of working with you.
- You do not have to change or stop doing anything you already do, just add this to it.

You want:

- More loans with less hassle
- Less haggling with customers over fees
- Larger commissions per loan
- Customer loyalty
- More time off without a drop in income
- Referrals generated automatically
- And you want to know if this system can deliver the goods!

Well, guess what? It can and does!

In fact, you will learn how one loan officer using the system generated 17 loans from one family within 3 months, using only the most basic techniques in the system!

For more info, visit: **ReferralsOnDemand.com**

"HOW TO GET AN ENTHUSIASTIC 'YES!' FROM REAL ESTATE AGENTS AND BROKERS, EVERY TIME YOU ASK FOR BUSINESS."

Working with just one average Realtor can put over $40,000 in your pocket year after year!

Read on to learn how you can get DOZENS of them
to call you,
without cold calling,
without rejection,
without donuts,
and without rate sheets.

A realtor called me the other day, and you won't believe what he said:

"Mr. Kamadia, another agent in my office works with you, and she told me this morning how she no longer has to spend any time following up on her leads. She also said how her business has increased as a direct result of working with you. I did over 4 million in sales last year and I would love to meet with you and discuss how we can work together."

He would never have called me if it wasn't for my simple, easy to use, almost-no-work-involved marketing system. My system gets dozens of Realtors to call me wanting me to help them increase their business. And because I help them make more money, they give me all their loans and leads. You can easily do the same thing I do.

My new system of getting Realtor business has been so successful, I had to hire another assistant!

I call my system **The Marketing To Agents Toolkit**. It's called a Toolkit because it has everything you need to attract, convert, and get business from realtors and real estate agents. The whole idea that makes the Toolkit so successful is simple. By giving Realtors what they want, they give me what I want. Sit up straight and pay attention now because here's the key: I offer Realtors something they want—they call me to get it. And when I give them what I promised, I show them something else, something that they cannot live without—and that they can have, only IF they work with me.

When they see what I have to offer, their eyes light up like 10-year-olds in a toy store, because they know it could easily double or triple their income in a few months.

Using this system you can easily work with 10, 20, 30 or more Realtors.

If you have ever been rejected by a Realtor, you need to keep reading!

Look how easy it is to use the Toolkit. (NO DONUTS OR RATE SHEETS.)

Step 1. Use my ads or letters to offer Realtors an information-filled "package" that will show them "How to Double Their Income in 90 Days."

Step 2. Once they call you to get this information (no cold-calling), you use the scripts provided to arrange a meeting with the agent in which you give them the "package."

Step 3. In the meeting you use the other set of scripts included to explain to them the benefits of your "Client Follow-Up System."

Step 4: If they don't agree to work with you right away (most do), you use the "Agent Follow Up System" until they do.

For the complete details visit:
MarketingToAgents.com

AFTER I GIVE YOU MY MOST PRIZED, PERSONALLY TESTED STRATEGIES FOR MAKING TRULY MASSIVE INCOME, IT'LL TAKE KRYPTONITE TO STOP YOU FROM OUT-EARNING EVERYBODY YOU KNOW—

In Fact, You May Want To Keep How Much Money You Make A Secret!

The Millionaire Loan Officer newsletter is written by someone who is and has been in almost every facet of the industry. The editor is Ameen Kamadia, President of Kamrock Publishing, mortgage consultant, coach, and author of this particular book. He is personally responsible for the marketing that has generated hundreds of millions in loan origination revenue.

He started from scratch in almost all his endeavors. He has paid his dues as a credit bureau manager, a real estate agent, a new mortgage broker, an internet marketing newbie, a real estate investor, and a direct marketing student of the masters. He started with little, and made his way to the top. Ameen can show you what works and what does not. Too many mortgage "gurus" keep spouting gimmicks to make themselves rich by selling their stuff. Doing what everyone else does will assure that you will never get ahead of the pack. Don't do what others have already failed at. Make it easier on yourself by doing only what has proven to work time and time again. And that is what you will learn in The Millionaire Loan Officer Newsletter.

continued on next page

The Name Is No Accident

Becoming a millionaire is not as hard as some make it out to be. And it is a lot easier if you have a millionaire mentor to show you the way.

Each issue of The Millionaire Loan Officer Newsletter is chock-full of tips, techniques, and strategies that will boost your income tremendously. Page after page of the newsletter is filled with information you can only get from someone who has been there before and is in the trenches everyday.

Every strategy promoted by Ameen has been tested in his own mortgage business. If it works, and only if it works, will he tell readers to do the same thing. Add in the strategies shared with Ameen by his coaching clients, and you have the best mortgage marketing minds sharing what is making them rich beyond their wildest dreams.

All this can be yours with a subscription to The Millionaire Loan Officer Newsletter. Most of the information that appears in the newsletter is available nowhere else. And it is available to you for just pennies a day.

Can you afford to waste time and money on marketing that does not work? If not, then you NEED this newsletter.

Are you new to the business and want to cut years off the learning curve? If yes, then you NEED this newsletter.

Are You Ready To Be a Millionaire Loan Officer?

For more info, visit:
MortgageBrokerTraining.com